AN ISLAND TO ONESELF

Tom Neale

AN ISLAND TO ONESELF

THE STORY OF SIX YEARS ON A DESERT ISLAND

THE QUALITY BOOK CLUB
121 CHARING CROSS ROAD
LONDON W.C.2.

FOR GEORGE MOORE TAGGART III
MY AMERICAN FRIEND IN
THE OLD TAHITI DAYS

© 1966 by Tom Neale
Printed in Great Britain
Collins Clear-Type Press
London and Glasgow

Contents

Contents

Author's Note

This is the story of six years which I spent alone, in two spells on an uninhabited coral atoll half a mile long and three hundred yards wide in the South Pacific. It was two hundred miles from the nearest inhabited island, and I first arrived there on October 7, 1952 and remained alone (with only two yachts calling) until June 24, 1954, when I was taken off ill after a dramatic rescue.

I was unable to return to the atoll until April 23, 1960 and this time I remained alone until December 27, 1963.

TOM NEALE

Tahiti and Rarotonga, 1964-1965

INTRODUCTION

by Noel Barber

For FOUR ROUGH DAYS I had sailed due east from
Samoa in a rusty old vessel called the *Manua Tele* which
I had chartered in Pago Pago. Our destination was
Suvarov atoll, a tiny group of islets in a coral reef nor-
mally uninhabited but where, it was said, a white man
had lived alone for five years.

When I awoke on the fifth morning, the swell had
gone, the *Manua Tele*'s engines were still, and the old
tub was rocking gently at anchor. I donned a pair of
shorts, picked up a tin of beer and some bananas and
went on deck.

Ahead of us the reef thrashed the water in a line
stretching for miles; beyond it, drenched in sun, was
man's most elusive dream, a coral island.

Suddenly, as the Samoan at the wheel searched for the
pass through the reef, I saw a flash of movement where
the palms met the coral, and a man bounded out and
started waving. Through the glasses I saw him run to a
tiny boat, push it into the water, and a few minutes later
he had a sail up to help him as he rowed towards the
Manua Tele. Within twenty minutes he was climbing
aboard with the agility of a boy of twenty.

"Not bad for fifty-eight," he grinned; and this was
my introduction to a man who had done what millions
of us dream of doing, but never seem to do. For Tom

Neale, a New Zealander, had left the world behind for
life alone on a coral island so remote from the trade
routes that he was fortunate if one ship a year called by
chance to disturb his solitude.

What had made him do it? Was he intelligent—
or was he slightly mad? He didn't *look* a crank, as he sat
there on the deck, the *Manua Tele* rolling gently in the
swell. Tall and spare, his skin was stained dark brown;
he wore tennis shoes, a pair of ragged shorts, ("Usually I
wear a strip of pareu, but I thought there might be women
aboard!") and a battered old hat. His greying hair was
close-cropped. But it was his eyes that fascinated me.
Brown and watchful—the alertness accentuated by the
wrinkles the sun had drawn on his burned face—they
were never still. They had a laugh in them, but they
were always restlessly watching—a cloud in the sky, the
Samoan mate's brown back, the size of a wave, me,
each time I spoke.

Though I am delighted that Tom has asked me to
write an introduction to his book, it is not my place to
describe the island and how he met the challenge of
living on it. Tom has done that in a story I have found
fascinating. I am more concerned with the man himself
—with perhaps some aspects of his character that he has
not put forward, for I found him very modest, quiet and
intelligent, with a wonderful sense of humour and a lively
curiosity about events in the world he had left behind.
No, this was no crank.

He kept a journal, and its pages were crammed with
neat, careful writing. He used an old-fashioned nib
—in itself an indication of a character far more fastidious
than I would have imagined; for any thoughts that Tom
Neale might have lowered his standards simply because
he was alone were quickly dispelled. Indeed, of all the
anomalies of Tom's island, nothing struck me so forcibly

as the sight of him carefully washing up; holding a glass to the light to be sure it was clean—all incredibly incongruous, for outside, the coconut palms rustled, the sea lapped on the beach, and beyond the reef the lonely immensity of the Pacific started rolling to the nearest coral atoll two hundred miles away.

But Tom was the most house-proud man I ever met. Every cup and saucer was in its right place. The dish-cloth was stretched to dry. When I dropped a bit of coconut shell on the veranda, he quickly kicked it away, and twice on that first day he swept out the hut with his home-made broom of palm fronds. And when he made his first cup of good tea for months with the tea I had brought him, he carefully heated the pot first.

"Even when I use old leaves over and over again, I always heat the pot first," he said, adding almost severely, "I *hate* tea out of a cold pot."

I can see him now after dinner, sitting on an old box, leaning forward, drawing an aimless pattern in the white coral dust, enjoying the sheer pleasure of talking, of forming words, for mine was the first ship he had seen for eight months.

But as he talked, I realised with something of a shock that though he was obviously pleased to see me, and was delighted with the stores I had brought him, he would not miss me when I left. He had never even bothered to inquire how long I intended to stay.

Only when I asked him the inevitable question "What made you do it?" was he silent for a long time, and I can remember the scene now on that long, black beautiful night; the hurricane lamp between us, Tom's mahogany-coloured face half lit, two cups and the empty teapot on the roughly hewn table, one of his cats sitting upright, still as an idol.

"Many people asked me that—even before I left to come here," he said finally, "and I must admit I've answered the question in many different ways; probably to get rid of them because I felt they would never *really* understand. Sometimes I've tried to put my feelings into words. But even then I would wonder, 'Is that really why I came?'

"The real truth is, you don't make decisions like this all at once. I'd been growing towards the idea for thirty years."

Then suddenly he added, half teasingly, "Don't go getting the wrong idea, though, and thinking I'm a hermit. Do I look like one?" He leaned forward. "I like people—I honestly do. I'm not just evading responsibilities. I suppose really—honestly—I don't quite know why I did come here in the first place."

We sat talking far into the night. The moon came up, silhouetting the *Manua Tele* framed in palms, reminding me of a scene in *Treasure Island* with the *Hispaniola* anchored off-shore. But that had been a beautiful island of violence; this was a paradise of peace. Everything was calm and still on the beach. Even for me, a casual visitor, the world had ceased to exist. Here was nothing but peace, for even nature was not hostile.

When the time came for me to leave Suvarov, something very curious happened. I had, in fact, rather dreaded the moment, possibly thinking of those endless embarrassing farewells on railway platforms; but when the actual moment arrived and the *Manua Tele*'s boat was ready to take me off the beach, Tom squeezed my hand firmly and said: "It's been wonderful seeing you, Noel, and I can't thank you enough for all the stores you brought."

I wondered how he felt, but I had no time to find out, for as the crew pushed the boat into the turquoise water, he loped back up the beach and vanished in the shade of the coconut palms. He never once looked back.

Was that quick, unemotional farewell a sign of inner contentment or was it a mask to hide his despair at being left alone?

I never knew until I read this book.

Part One

THE YEARS OF
WAITING

1. Wanderlust in the Sun

I WAS FIFTY when I went to live alone on Suvarov, after thirty years of roaming the Pacific, and in this story I will try to describe my feelings, try to put into words what was, for me, the most remarkable and worthwhile experience of my whole life.

I chose to live in the Pacific islands because life there moves at the sort of pace which you feel God must have had in mind originally when He made the sun to keep us warm and provided the fruits of the earth for the taking; but though I came to know most of the islands, for the life of me I sometimes wonder what it was in my blood that had brought me to live among them. There was no history of wanderlust in my family that I knew of—other than the enterprise which had brought my father, who was born in Aylesbury, Buckinghamshire, out to New Zealand after serving with the 17th Lancers. By the time he met my mother, who came of sound pioneering stock, he had become a company secretary. And so I was born in Wellington, though while I was still a baby we moved to Greymouth in New Zealand's South Island, where my father was appointed paymaster to the state coal mines. Here we remained until I was about seven, when the family—I had two brothers and three sisters—moved to Timaru on the opposite side of South Island.

It was a change for the better. My maternal grand-

SUWARROW and NASSAU are the least important of the northern atolls. Nassau lies close to Pukapuka and, in 1961, supported 109 people from Pukapuka, engaged in copra making. Suwarrow is a bird sanctuary of 100 acres and is inhabited by Mr. Tom Neale, a New Zealander who prefers a lonely atoll life.

How To Reach The Cook Islands

The New Zealand Government's 2,750 ton, 40 passenger motor vessel, *Moana Roa*, makes regular monthly voyages from Auckland to Rarotonga. A limited number of berths from and to New Zealand are available during the winter months for *bona fide* tourists. Calls are made at some of the Cook's outer islands when cargo warrants. Current information can be obtained from the Department of Island Territories, Wellington, and offices of the Union Steamship Co. of New Zealand Ltd.

ISLAND	Population 1961.	Distance and Direction from Rarotonga Miles		POSI
RAROTONGA	8,676	-	-	21° 12'06"S
AITUTAKI	2,582	140	N	18°51'45"S
MANGAIA	1,877	110	ESE	21°54'30"S
ATIU	1,266	116	NEbyE	19°59'35"S
MAUKE	785	150	ENE	20°08'30"S
MITIARO	307	142	NEbyE	19°51' S
MANUAE (Hervey Is.)	18	124	NNE	19° 15' S
TAKUTEA		118	NE	19°48'35"S
MANIHIKI	1,006	650	NbyW	10°25'20"S
PUKAPUKA	718	715	NWbyN	10°53' S
PENRHYN	628	737	NbyE	8°59'45"S
PALMERSTON	86	270	NW	18°04' S
RAKAHANGA	319	674	NbyW	10°02'30"S
NASSAU	109	673	NWbyN	11°33'20"S
SUWARROW	1	513	NNW	13°14'40"S

Part of a page from *Maps of the Cook Islands* issued by the Rarotonga Survey Department, with a reference to me on the last line

mother owned twenty acres of land only five miles out of
Timaru and here we settled down, my father commuting
to his new office either by bicycle, trap or on horseback,
while I went to the local school where (with all due
modesty) I was good enough in reading, geography and
arithmetic to merit a rapid move from Standard One
to Standard Three.

Looking back, I imagine the real clue to my future
aspirations lay in the fact that it always seemed absolutely natural that I should go to sea. I cannot remember
ever contemplating any other way of life and there was
no opposition from my parents when I announced I
would like to join the New Zealand Navy. My real
ambition was to become a skilled navigator, but when
my father took me to Auckland Naval Base to sign on, I
was dismayed to discover that already I was too old at
eighteen and a half to be apprenticed as a seaman.

It was a bitter disappointment, but I had set my
heart on a seafaring career and did the next best thing.
Signing on as an apprentice engineer meant starting right
at the bottom—and I mean at the bottom—as a stoker,
although I didn't mind because the job, however menial,
would give me a chance to see something of the Pacific.

I spent four years in the New Zealand Navy before
buying myself out, and I only left because of a nagging
desire to see more of the world than the brief glimpses we
obtained beyond the confining, narrow streets of the ports
where we docked. And our visits were dictated by naval
necessity—simple things like routine patrols or defective
boilers—so that I saw Papeete but never Tahiti; Apia but
never Samoa; Nukualofa but never Tonga. It was the
islands I always longed to see, not a vista of dock cranes
nor the sleazy bars which one can find in every maritime
corner of the world.

For the next few years I wandered from island to

island. Sometimes I would take a job for a few months as a fireman on one of the slow, old, inter-island tramps. When I tired of this, I would settle down for a spell, clearing bush or planting bananas. There was always work, and there was always food. And it was only now that I really came to know and love the islands strung like pearls across the South Pacific—Manihiki at dawn as the schooner threads its way through the pass in the reef; Papeete at sunset with the Pacific lapping up against the main street; the haze on the coconut palms of Puka Puka; the clouds above Moorea with its jagged silhouette of extinct volcanoes; Pago Pago, where Somerset Maugham created the character of Sadie Thompson, and where you can still find the Rainmaker's Hotel; Apia, where, I was later told, Michener was inspired to create Bloody Mary and where Aggie Grey's Hotel welcomes guests with a large whisky and soda.

I loved them all, and it was ten years before I returned to New Zealand in 1931. I was then twenty-eight and when I reached Timaru I telephoned my father at his office.

"Who's that?" he asked.

"Tom."

"Which Tom?"

"Your Tom!" I replied.

At first he could hardly believe it. But before long he was at the station to fetch me in his car. The old man looked much the same as I remembered him, as did my mother—but my brothers and sisters had grown so much that at first I scarcely recognised them. Ten years is a long time, but before long I was back in the family routine as though I had been away hardly more than a month. Yet, somehow, I remained an outsider in my own mind. I had seen too much, done so much, existed under a succession of such utterly different circumstances, that at times I would catch myself looking at my mother sitting placidly in her favourite chair and think to myself, "Is it really possible that for all these years while I've been seeing the world, she has sat there each evening apparently content?"

I stayed for some months, doing odd jobs, but then I was off again, and I knew this time where I wanted to go, for of all the islands one beckoned more than any other. This was Moorea, the small French island off Tahiti, and it was here that finally I settled—or thought I had—in an island of dramatic beauty, with its jagged peaks of blue and grey rising from the white beaches to awesome pinnacles against the blue sky. It is a small island in which, however, everything seems to be a little larger than life. It is an island of plenty. I could walk along the twisting, narrow coast road and pick guavas, coconuts or paw-paws and pineapples and nobody would be angry. The French, who had superimposed their wonderful way of life on the people, took care that Moorea should remain unspoiled.

Only one boat a day made the twelve-mile trip from Papeete and passed through the narrow channel in the barrier reef. And—when I was there, anyway—providing a man behaved himself, he was left alone, and I preferred it that way. I had to work—indeed, I wanted to work—and there was always bush to be cleared, copra to be prepared, fish to be caught. I really wanted for nothing, and I remember saying to myself one beautiful evening after swimming in the lagoon, "Neale," (I always call myself Neale when I talk to myself), "this is the nearest thing on earth to paradise."

Life was incredibly cheap. A bullock was slaughtered twice a week and we were able to buy the meat at fourpence a pound. Within a short time of settling down the natives had built me a comfortable two-roomed shack for which I paid them a bag of sugar and a small case of corned beef. Life was as simple as that. I had my own garden, a wood-burning stove, plenty of vegetables, fruit and fish.

My living expenses never came to more than £1 a week—often the total was less—because from the moment I left the Navy I had made up my mind to "batch"—in other words, look after myself completely; do my own washing, cooking, mending, and never move anywhere without being entirely equipped to fend for myself. It is a decision I have stuck to all my life. Even now, I am never without my own mattress, sheets, pillows, blankets, cutlery, crockery, kitchen utensils and a battered old silver teapot.

Even as I write, the "housewife" which the Navy gave me the day I joined up is not far out of reach. It is in itself a symbol of years of "batching" which has saved me a fortune. Mine was a simple existence. No furnished rooms to rent, no meals to buy. My only luxury was buying books.

I was very happy in Moorea. I quickly learned to speak Tahitian, I made one or two friends, I worked fairly hard, I read a great deal. My taste in literature is catholic—anything from Conrad or Defoe to a Western; the only thing I demand is an interesting book in bed last thing at night.

It was in Moorea that I first stumbled on the works of the American writer Robert Dean Frisbie, who was to have such an important influence on my life. Frisbie had settled in the Pacific, and had written several volumes about the islands which I read time and time again, though it never entered my head then that one day we should be friends.

I might have stayed in Moorea for ever, but around 1940, at a moment when I thought myself really happy, a character came into my life who was to change it in a remarkable way. This was Andy Thompson, the man who led me to Frisbie, captain of a hundred-ton island schooner called the *Tiare Taporo*—the "Lime Flower."

I met Andy on a trip to Papeete and immediately liked him. He was bluff, hearty and a good friend, though after that first meeting months would sometimes pass before we met again, for we had to wait until the *Tiare Taporo* called at Papeete. We never corresponded.

I was astounded, therefore, to receive a letter from him one day. It must have been early in 1943. Andy was a man used to commanding a vessel and never wasted words. He simply wrote: "Be ready. I've got a job for you in the Cook Islands."

At that time I didn't particularly *want* a job in the Cook Islands and Andy didn't even tell me what the job was. Yet when the *Tiare Taporo* arrived in Papeete a few weeks later, I was waiting. And because I sailed back with him I was destined to meet Frisbie, who in turn "led" me to Suvarov.

To this day, I do not know why I returned with Andy— particularly as the job he had lined up involved me in running a store on one of the outer islands belonging to the firm which owned Andy's schooner. The regular storekeeper was due to go on leave and I was supposed to relieve him. On his return, I gathered, I would be sent on as a sort of permanent relief storekeeper to the other islands in the Cooks. I suppose, subconsciously, I must have been ready for a change of environment. Nonetheless, I didn't find the prospect entirely attractive.

First, I had to go to Rarotonga and here, within two days of arriving, I met Frisbie.

Since this man's influence was to bear deeply on my life, I must describe him. Frisbie was a remarkable man. Some time before I met him, his beautiful native wife had died, leaving him with four young children. He loved the islands; his books about them had been well reviewed but had not, as far as I could learn, made him much money. Not that that worried him, for his life was writing and he had the happy facility for living from one day to the next with, apparently, hardly a care in the world. He was, he told me, an old friend of Andy's, and any friend of Andy's was a friend of his. It was Sunday morning and, unknown to me, Andy had invited us both for lunch.

I could not have known then what momentous consequences this meeting was to have. None of us suspected it then but Frisbie had only a few more years to live (he was to die of tetanus), and on that Sunday morning I saw in front of me a tall, thin man of about forty-five with an intelligent but emaciated face. He looked ill, but I remember how his eagerness and enthusiasm mounted as he started to talk about "our" islands and told me of his desire to write more books about them. We liked each other on sight, which surprised me, for I do not make friends easily; and it was after lunch—washed down with a bottle of Andy's excellent rum—that Frisbie first mentioned Suvarov.

Of course, I had heard of this great lagoon, with its coral reef stretching nearly fifty miles in circumference, but I had never been there, for it was off the trade routes, and shipping rarely passed that way.

Because its reef is submerged at high tide—leaving only a line of writhing white foam to warn the navigator of its perils—Suvarov, however, is clearly marked on all maps. Yet Suvarov is not the name of an island, but of an atoll, and the small islets inside the lagoon each have their own names. The islets vary in size from Anchorage, the largest, which is half a mile long, to One Tree Island, the smallest, which is merely a mushroom of coral. The atoll lies almost in the centre of the Pacific, five hundred and thirteen miles north of Rarotonga, and the nearest inhabited island is Manihiki, two hundred miles distant.

That afternoon Frisbie entranced me, and I can see him now on the veranda, the rum bottle on the big table between us, leaning forward with that blazing characteristic earnestness, saying to me, "Tom Neale, Suvarov is the most beautiful place on earth, and no man has really lived until he has lived there."

Fine words, I thought, but not so easy to put into action.

"Of course, you must remember," he broke in, "there's a war on, and at present Suvarov is inhabited."

This I knew—for two New Zealanders with three native helpers were stationed on Anchorage in Suvarov's lagoon. These "coast-watchers" kept an eye open for ships or aircraft in the area, and would report back any movement to headquarters by radio.

"But they'd probably be glad to see you—or even me," added Frisbie with a touch of irony.

I got up for it was time to leave. And as I said good-bye to this tall, thin man whose face and eyes seemed to burn with enthusiasm, I said, and the words and sigh came straight from the heart, "That's the sort of place for me."

"Well—if you feel that way about it, why don't you go there?" he retorted.

Storekeeping was not a very arduous job and I soon fell into my new life. My first "posting" took me to Atiu— a small island with rounded, flat-topped hills, and fertile valleys filled with oranges, coconuts and paw-paw; all of it less than seven thousand acres, each one of them exquisite and forever beckoning. From there I moved on to Puka Puka—"the Land of Little Hills"—where seven hundred people lived and produced copra.

The pattern of my life hardly varied, irrespective of the island on which I happened to be relieving the local storekeeper.

Each morning I would make my breakfast, open up the store and wait for the first native customers in the square functional warehouse with its tin roof. The walls were lined with shelves of flour, tea, coffee beans, tinned goods, cloth, needles—everything which one didn't *really* need at all in an island already overflowing with fruit and fish! No wonder that as I was shuttled from one outer island to another, I soon discovered that storekeeping was not the life for me, though it did have its compensations.

As long as I kept my stock and accounts in good order, I had a fair amount of leisure, which I occupied by reading. In some stores we carried supplies of paperback books so even my browsing cost me nothing, providing I didn't dirty the covers. I was batching, of course, and each store had free quarters so I was able to save a little money, especially as in some of the smaller islands the white population could be counted on the fingers of one hand.

Mine was, in every sense of the word, a village store. One moment I would be selling flour, the next I would be advising a mother how to cure her baby's cough. I carried an alarming assortment of medicines (always very popular) as well as a jumble of odds and ends ranging from spectacles to cheap binoculars, from brightly decorated tin trunks to lengths of rusty chain. I had drums of kerosene for the smoking lamps of the village, lines and hooks for the fishermen who, more often than not, would try to buy these with their latest catch of parrot fish or crays.

I came to be something of a "doctor" and village counsellor, and this I did find a rewarding part of my job, for in the really small islands I was often the only man to whom the people could turn for help. In an indirect way, I was money-lender, too—because I alone had the power to judge the worth of a man's credit against the future price of copra, and many is the bolt of calico I have sold against nuts still on the tree.

The really sad conclusion about my life as a storekeeper is that I *might* have enjoyed it had the store been in Tahiti or Moorea or had I never met Frisbie and been fired with the dream of going to Suvarov, for my yearnings were not desperate ones; I didn't spend all my days mooning about. But always in the back of my mind was the vague feeling, "What a bore life is! Wouldn't it be wonderful if for once I could see what life is like on an uninhabited island."

As it was, I seemed to spend my time waiting for the inter-island schooner which, every now and then, would lie off the island, giving the people a reason for wakening for a few hours out of their languid torpor while my stores were unloaded. Occasionally, Andy would sail in in the *Tiare Taporo*, then we would spend an evening on *my* veranda.

It was an uneventful, placid existence and though I should have been content enough, I soon disliked it intensely. Why, then, did I remain for years as a storekeeper moving around from island to island? The main reason was that every time I was transferred, I had to return through Rarotonga and so met up with Frisbie again.

Then we would talk far into the night about Suvarov (and the other islands of the Pacific) and occasionally, when the rum bottle was low, I was able to persuade him to read the latest passages he had written. He had a deep compelling voice, and talked with as much enthusiasm as he wrote. And towards the end of each evening—and often "the end" only came when the dawn was streaking over the red tin roofs of Raro—we always came back to Suvarov.

"Do you think I'll *ever* get there?" I asked one night.

"Why not?" answered Frisbie, "though probably you'll have to wait until the war's over." I remember we were sitting together sipping a last beer on a visit to Rarotonga, "but *then*—there's no reason why you shouldn't go—that is, providing you equip yourself properly. Suvarov may be beautiful, but it not only *looks* damn fragile, it *is* damn fragile—and I should know."

There was no need to elaborate. I already knew that in the great hurricane of 1942, sixteen of the twenty-two islets in the lagoon had literally been washed away within a matter of hours. Frisbie had been trapped on Anchorage with his four small children and the coast-watchers during this hurricane. He had saved the children's lives by lashing them in the forks of tamanu trees elastic enough to bend with the wind until the violence of the storm was spent.

I did not see Frisbie again for some time, but we corresponded regularly, and one day when I was feeling particularly low, I picked up his book, *The Island of Desire*. When I came to the second half I discovered it was all about Suvarov; how he had lived on the island with his children, how he had been caught in that great hurricane. I was enthralled and his descriptions were so vivid that no sooner had I finished the book than I sat down and wrote to him. "One of these days," I wrote in my sloping, eager hand, "that's where I'm going to live."

Frisbie replied, a half joking letter in which he suggested

"Let's both go. You can live on Motu Tuo and I can live on Anchorage, and we can visit each other."

It made sense. For like me, Frisbie was naturally a solitary man. Like me, he never had much money and yet, sadly, we were never to see the island together. In fact, Frisbie was never to see Suvarov again before he died in 1948.

There was another important reason for remaining in the Cooks. If ever I *did* go to Suvarov—if ever I had the luck or courage to "go it alone"—I would have to leave from Rarotonga, for Suvarov is in the Cook Islands, and though the inter-island trading schooners rarely passed near the atoll, there might one day be an occasion when a ship would sail close enough to the island to be diverted. But only from Raro.

This is exactly what happened. Suddenly, in 1945, there came an opportunity to visit Suvarov for two days. It was Andy who broke the news to me in Rarotonga. He was under orders, he told me, to take the *Tiare Taporo* round the islands, calling in at Suvarov with stores for the coast-watchers there, on his way back from Manihiki.

"I need an engineer for this trip," he said off-handedly, as though he did not know how much I longed to see the island. "Care to come along?"

I was aboard the *Tiare* before Andy had time to change his mind!

When we sailed a few days later, Andy and I were the only Europeans aboard amongst a crew of eight Cook Islanders. We set off for the Northern Cooks—Puka Puka, Penrhyn, Manihiki—which are all low-lying atolls quite different from the Southern Cooks which are always known as the "High Islands."

It was a pleasant, leisurely trip. I can imagine no more perfect way of seeing the South Pacific than from the deck of a small schooner. Life moved at an even, un-hurried pace. I did not have much work for the *Tiare* carried sail and the engine was seldom needed. Our normal routine was to sail for a few days until we reached an atoll, lay off-shore, discharging cargo, take on some copra and then sail off again into the beautiful blue Pacific with white fleecy clouds filling the sky above.

The night before we reached Suvarov, we lay well off the atoll without even sighting it, for Andy, a good navigator, had no intention of risking his ship during the hours of darkness. All through the night we could hear the faint, faraway boom of the swells breaking on Suvarov's reef. Though there was no moon, it was clear and starry, and I stood on deck for a long time, listening, filled with an emotion I cannot even attempt to describe, until finally I fell asleep dreaming of tomorrow.

Dawn brought perfect weather and we began to approach the atoll at first light, though it lay so flat that for a long time we could not make out the land ahead. We had a good wind and full sail, and the *Tiare* must have been making four knots without her engines as I stood on the cabin top, the only sound the lap of the water and the creaking of wood, shading my eyes until at last I caught my first glimpse of Suvarov—the pulsating, creamy foam of the reef thundering before us for miles, and a few clumps of palm trees silhouetted against the blue sky, the clumps widely separated on the islets that dotted the enormous, almost circular stretch of reef.

The air was shimmering under a sun already harsh as Andy took the *Tiare* towards the pass, and Anchorage started to take a more distinct shape. I could make out the white beach now, an old broken-down wharf—a relic of the days when attempts had been made to grow copra on the island—and then some figures waving on the beach.

From the south end a great flock of screaming frigate birds rose angrily into the air, black and wheeling, waiting for the smaller terns to catch fish so they could steal them.

How puny the islets seemed in the vast rolling emptiness of the Pacific! Frisbie had called them fragile but they were more than that. To me they looked almost forlorn, so that it seemed amazing they could have survived the titanic forces of nature which have so often wiped out large islands. Had they been rugged, then survival would have been easier to appreciate, but none of the islets ahead of us in the lagoon was more than ten or fifteen feet above sea level, so that only the tops of the coconut trees proclaimed their existence.

The chop of the sea ceased, for now we were in the lagoon, and it was as though the *Tiare* were floating on vast pieces of coloured satin. We edged towards Anchorage very slowly through a sea so still that our slight ripple hardly disturbed it. Like many South Pacific islets, Anchorage—lying just inside the lagoon—is subterraneously joined to the main reef by a submerged "causeway" of coral. And so, as I looked down into the water, I thought I had never seen so many colours in my life as the vivid blues, greens and even pinks that morning; no painter could have imitated those patterns formed by underwater coral at differing depths.

Then the anchor rattled down. We put a ship's boat overboard and a few minutes later I was wading ashore through the warm, still water towards the blinding white beach.

Common politeness made me greet the five men living there—each of them desperately anxious to go home as soon as possible!—but as soon as I decently could, I went off alone, and on that first day I took a spear and my machete—a French one I had bought in

Tahiti, more slender and pointed than those of the Cook Islands—and went along the reef, spearing the plentiful fish I discovered in the reef pools and so lazy that one could hardly miss them.

In the evening, I had supper with the coast-watchers and looked over their shack with the secret, questing eyes of a man wondering if one day he would inherit it. It seemed ideal. The tanks were full of good water, and when I went for a stroll I discovered a fine garden they had made out of a wilderness.

The watchers were only anxious to leave. How different are men's attitudes to life! They were agreeable, cheerful and noisy—and delighted with the stores we had brought them—but theirs was a forced gaiety, hiding their anger that war should have played them such a dirty trick as turning them into castaways on a desert island.

On the second day, Andy and I took a ship's boat to the islet of Motu Tuo six miles across the lagoon, where the native boys caught coconut crabs and fish and lit a fire to cook our picnic lunch.

And when lunch was over, I turned to Andy and said simply, but with utter conviction, "Andy, now I know this is the place I've been looking for all this time."

It was to take me seven more years before my dream came true. Seven long years before another vessel from Rarotonga passed anywhere near the island, seven years during which I reached middle age. Perhaps it was this consciousness of time passing, perhaps this and the dreariness of my job that brought an increasing heaviness of heart which I only managed to struggle against by clinging obstinately to the hope that I would one day get back to the island.

In 1952 my opportunity came. Dick Brown, an independent trader in Rarotonga, had gone into the shipping business after the war, buying a long, narrow submarine chaser of less than a hundred tons which he had converted into an inter-island trader. She was called the *Mahurangi*, and quite by chance I heard that on her next trip she was going north to Palmerston Island and then to Manihiki. I did not need a map to know that the course passed right by Suvarov.

In all my years in the Cooks, I had never heard of a trading vessel sailing this direct route; it was an opportunity which might never come my way again.

I totted up my finances. I had saved £79. I went to Dick and asked when he was sailing.

"In two weeks," he replied.

"How much would it cost to divert on the way to Manihiki and take me to Suvarov?"

He scratched his head, figuring.

"Thirty quid."

It seemed a lot of money, especially when the *Mahurangi* must pass almost within sight of Suvarov and could have dropped me off with little trouble. But diverting a vessel is always expensive and I did not argue.

"Done!" I said, and we shook hands on it.

I had just two weeks to gather together everything I thought a man would need to survive on an uninhabited coral atoll. Two weeks—and £49.

2. *Shopping List for a Desert Island*

THREE MINUTES . . . after so many years of waiting. Only three minutes to settle my passage, and the whole transaction concluded in an almost comically casual fashion.

I walked slowly back to the unfurnished room I was renting for 7s. 6d. a week in the valley behind Raro, praying I would not meet anybody; I had to be alone —just for a little while. I was not thinking—not yet— of the dozens of preparations which I must make within a very short time. Instead, as I walked home in the hot sunlight, my mind went back to that day with Andy on the *Tiare Taporo*, when he had edged into the lagoon, and I had had my first real impression of Anchorage. I could see it in my mind's eye now as I walked along and could still hardly believe that in a little over a couple of weeks I was going to be back there again. How excited Frisbie would have been. But poor Frisbie had been dead now for four years.

In my room I filled the kettle and made some tea on my primus, but was unable to bring myself to eat anything. My first overwhelming excitement was replaced now by hundreds of different jangling thoughts. For no reason I suddenly thought, "I mustn't forget fish hooks." In this daze I actually wasted several minutes mentally wrangling as to whether or not I ought to take any baking powder. Tea over, I went to wash up, and found myself saying almost crossly, "Neale, you'll need some new dishcloths."

I had only a fortnight before I sailed and there was so much to do. Nor could I turn to my friends for advice, for after all what would they know about living on a desert island? Even Andy was away at sea. Now the great moment had come, I was alone.

And maybe this was the best way, because once I calmed down, I discovered I really knew exactly what I would need. It was just a matter of getting things sorted out in my mind, so that the sudden thoughts that kept rushing in—like "I must get a crowbar!"—"How will I stop my tea going fusty?"—were pigeonholed in some sort of order.

I forced myself to concentrate on the island. I knew the coast-watchers had left some years ago, but I remembered now that they had had a flat-bottomed boat almost like a punt—and the chances were it would still be there. But would it be seaworthy? I made a mental note to buy a few copper nails.

I do not know how long I sat there—probably a couple of hours—whilst I jotted down the most vital items on an old bit of paper. But oddly enough, once I had got up and returned to the familiar world outside my shack, I never needed that piece of paper again. For my requirements now seemed written like a list in my mind where I suppose they had probably been accumulating subconsciously throughout all the years of waiting.

I was not afraid. That I can honestly say. Perhaps I was a little overawed by the challenge I had taken on. I *was* fifty now. And this dream of mine had been essentially a dream of youth. Was I too old now to turn this dream into successful reality? I flattered myself I was still in excellent shape, but there was no doubt that physical hardship would fall more heavily on me than it would have done twenty years ago; and then there was the possibility of falling ill . . . .

By the following day, however, I was back to normal— and I started as efficiently as I could to make an inventory of my possessions. I still have it on faded pieces of paper, dated August 1952. There are several lists; one headed "Personal Effects," another "The Kai Room" ("Kai" is the native word for eating, so my kai room list contained all the things I used for eating and cooking). The third list was headed "Tools."

How well I remember my very first purchase. It was a sack of Australian flour, from a shipment which had just arrived. This was a rare luxury in Raro as we naturally bought everything we could from New Zealand, but I had cooked with Australian flour from time to time and knew from experience that it would keep much longer than the local brand.

I also knew that once the news of its arrival got around, there would be a run on it, for the South Seas stores are really more like warehouses than shops, and when shipments of new lines arrive to be piled up against the shelves of the barn-like buildings, everyone in town rushes to buy. So I was down at Raro's "shopping district" as soon as the stores opened, asking the assistant at Donald's, whom I had known for years, "Any of the Australian flour left?"

"Sure, Tom," he replied. "How much—a couple of pounds?"

"How much is it?"

"Sixpence a pound."

"Oh well," I pretended to hesitate, secretly enjoying the joke, "Might as well take a fifty-pound sack!"

He nearly dropped it; and at that moment the wife and daughter of a Government official came in, and stared in astonishment at the sight of Neale buying a whole sack of flour, so on the spur of the moment I added, as casually as I could, "While I'm here, I'd better take a seventy-pound bag of sugar!"

After that, the news was soon round Raro—even though I said very little myself. But you can't keep secrets on an island of only eight thousand people, especially when I —normally so careful—began to buy goods by the sackful.

Most of the stores like Donald's or the Cook Islands Trading Company—both famous island firms—had their functional buildings grouped on or near Main Road between the solid white building of the Residency and Avarua harbour, and now I started shopping in earnest.

I came in for a lot of good-natured banter. After all, had been on friendly terms with some of the assistants for a long time, and the sight of me staggering out of Donald's with enough coffee beans to last a year was bound to provoke curiosity or mirth.

At least I faced no problems as far as my "personal effects" were concerned. These consisted of a couple of pairs of long trousers, a few singlets, three or four light shirts, two pairs of khaki shorts, three pareus (a sort of native sarong), two pairs of sandals and a raincoat. Naturally, I also had my Navy "housewife," a razor, an old shaving-brush, a toothbrush, and a pocket-knife.

My sleeping gear was simple, although you could hardly call it extensive. I had my kapok mattress, a pair of sheets, an ex-Navy blanket, another lighter blanket, two pillows, two pillow slips and two towels. I planned to roll the whole lot up in the mattress, which I would wrap round with some old pandanus matting for protection when the time came to sail.

I needed only a few other personal effects. I invested in

thread and needles for my "housewife"; I bought twenty-four razor blades which would last me some years, for I had long since learned that by sharpening them in a glass under water, I was able to use the same blade for three months or so. I thought I would probably shave twice a week, though I received several amiable suggestions that it would be cheaper—and more in keeping with my illustrious predecessor, Robinson Crusoe—to grow a beard. The same assistant who sold me the blades also asked me why I didn't have all my teeth out before leaving instead of wasting money on the four tubes of toothpaste I bought.

Yet the interesting thing is that during the fortnight there was nothing malicious or sarcastic in any of the humour. Nobody was trying to take a rise out of me; indeed, I had a feeling, as I suddenly became a sort of local curiosity, that most people were secretly envying me.

I remember going into Donald's and ordering two pairs of rubber-soled tennis shoes which I knew would be necessary to protect my feet when fishing on the coral reef. The salesman was an old pal of mine, and after saying jokingly, "Want anybody to carry your bags?" he added quite earnestly, "Two pairs isn't enough, Tom. You know the islands better than I do, but let's face it, you've always been near a store. What's going to happen when these shoes wear out—or if you lose them?" He was right—and I bought six pairs. It turned out to be a very wise decision.

I planned to pack my clothes in an old suitcase and an equally ancient but serviceable Gladstone bag. Wonderful bags, the Gladstones—they have a great capacity for stretching and into this one, besides my clothes, I tucked a supply of writing materials; two bottles of ink, half a dozen spare nibs, some paper and envelopes, two big Collins "Trader" diaries—a page to a day—and a calendar.

As the day of departure drew nearer, I paid almost daily visits to the *Mahurangi* which lay in Avarua harbour. I knew most of the Cook Island crew—indeed, one or two of them had sailed with me on other vessels—and I would stop and chat with them, perhaps drawn towards them by a common love of the sea, perhaps because I knew they would be taking me to Suvarov, perhaps because I needed some reassurance; and when Dick Brown, who regarded my frequent visits with amusement, asked one morning, "What's the trouble, Tom? Scared we'll leave without you?" I suddenly felt a little cross and answered seriously and surlily, "You can't. I've paid my passage money."

For the truth is, I probably *was* a little frightened. It was never a predominant emotion—I never for a moment considered abandoning the enterprise—but, well, there were the odd times when I wondered if I weren't a bit too old, and there were times when I asked myself if I really realised what life would be like without another human being to talk to for months on end.

I would hardly have been natural had I not occasionally felt this way, but the flashes of despondency always passed quickly. Quite apart from the fact that I had a great deal to do, I now became quite touched by the way people I hardly counted as friends rallied round. One day, staggering home with several parcels, a woman I knew only slightly offered me a lift in her car, and when we reached my shack in the valley she said, "Tom, I envy you. It's the sort of thing everybody would love to do. I've got a very good barometer I never use— I'd like to lend it to you."

It was exactly what I wanted but could not afford, and I accepted it gratefully. Then when I had difficulty finding two heavy strips of flat-iron which I wanted as firebars to rest on stones, the P.W.D., (Public Works Department) for whom I had worked occasionally, offered to give me a couple. A Government department!

I even had more than one proposition from the ladies. And I may say that I was tempted, for the Cook Island women are not only handsome but wonderfully adaptable, used to hard work, and can turn their hands to anything. Frisbie had found great happiness with his native wife, so when one woman of about thirty, the sister of a Cook Island friend, quite seriously offered to come (adding ingenuously, "You don't need to marry me!") I definitely considered the possibility.

However, I decided against it. I had been batching so long I really didn't need a woman. And, perhaps most of all, the prospect of being cooped up with a woman who might eventually annoy me, of being imprisoned with her—like a criminal on Devil's Island, without hope of escape—made me shudder. I would be better off as a middle-aged bachelor.

Curiously, those of my acquaintances who (sometimes facetiously and with sly winks) suggested I should take a woman to Suvarov all seemed most concerned lest I should fall ill alone, and regarded a "wife" as a necessity in case she had to play the role of nurse.

Indeed, the most persistent question posed by my friends during these last two hectic weeks was, "Aren't you afraid of illness?"

Was I? I don't think so. I cannot deny that occasionally a moment of apprehension flitted across my mind, particularly at the thought of an unexpected accident such as a broken limb. But any fears were fleeting. I couldn't *allow* myself to be afraid, otherwise I might just as well go back to storekeeping. And I have always been fit, apart from the odd dose of fever. My eyesight was good, and as far as accidents were concerned, men like myself who are used to living very close to nature gradually acquire a special sort of protective instinct when using tools like saws or axes, or heating metal or climbing trees. It is the tenderfoot who usually cuts or burns himself. Automatically, I was in the habit of taking far greater care than the normal man.

I was, however, worried about the possibility of toothache, for that was something I could not control. I had had an upper plate for several years, but I went to the dentist and told him to take out as many of my bottom teeth as he wanted! It says much for my simple life that he only extracted one—and I have never had toothache.

I had to take some medical precautions, but I could not afford to take a really extensive kit, much as I would have liked to have it. Drugs cost so much. So I had to content myself with plenty of bandages, sticking-plaster, Germolene, a supply of Band-Aid, a little cotton wool, one bottle of Vaseline and a half-pint bottle of Mertholiate, plenty of antiseptic, some sulphur thiazole (M & B) tablets for fevers. I bought no aspirin because I never get headaches.

Of course, I did not spend one day buying food, or another selecting pots and pans. Like any housewife, I became a familiar figure in the local stores, carrying my shopping lists and buying whatever I needed from the heaped shelves and counters. I used to stagger home with my purchases, tick them off on my list and then pack them in a motley assembly of variously sized parcels, making a note of the contents of each packet.

I spent a great deal of time on my food list. I knew I would never starve on Suvarov, for I expected to find coconuts, bananas, paw-paw and breadfruit, in addition to unlimited fish and crayfish. I also knew that the coast-watchers had kept fowls, though I could not be certain if there would be any left.

But obviously a diet consisting of only island produce was going to be monotonous, and since I had £49 I saw no reason for not laying out a substantial part of it on supplies that would at least tide me over until my garden was producing.

I had a pretty good idea of what I wanted, for after all I had been cooking my own meals for half a lifetime and I went from store to store buying the different basic foods. By the time I had finished, my stock of purchases, piled up in my shack, was not unimpressive.

I decided quite deliberately to spend some of my money on gastronomic luxuries which I really did not need, for though I had proved many times that I could live on native or island food, I had noticed over the years how the sudden switch to such a spartan diet tended to make me a little depressed. Breadfruit and coconuts sound all very well in adventure stories, but nobody can deny they are monotonous. I felt I should ease my way into the new life ahead of me by starting out with some of the foods I enjoyed.

After all, I didn't *really* know what lay in the future. I flattered myself I would never be lonely, but how could I tell? I remember having a beer one evening with a friend, and when I pooh-poohed his suggestion that I might be bored with my own company, he pointed out quite seriously, "I know you enjoy being on your own, Tom, but remember you've always had *somebody* around —if only to call them a damned nuisance! What's going to happen if you're alone—and lonely? Nobody to shout at—not even an enemy!"

He was right, of course. How could I tell what I would feel in circumstances which I had only so far imagined? Well, at least I could get some good food to cheer me up if I felt too low. I went down to Donald's the next morning and promptly bought a dozen one-pound tins of jam and a dozen tins of sweetened condensed milk!

I already had my flour and sugar, a forty-pound bag of coffee beans, and now I bought a forty-pound tin of Suva biscuits, also known as "cabin bread", which I had chewed for years on the inter-island boats where it was always produced when the flour gave out—as it regularly did. I bought it for the same reason—to use when my flour gave out, or went bad. These biscuits were about four inches square, about ten to the pound. I chose my sealed tin with great care, checking that no seams were broken or punctured, for tins often arrived from Suva in bad condition.

Though I hoped there would be fowls on the island, I felt I had to take some meat with me, so I bought two dozen tins of bully beef to eat on special occasions, together with ten pounds of beef dripping which I sealed up with sticking plaster in an old sweet tin. I became a regular cadger of old sweet tins—even though sometimes I had to pay a shilling each for them. I needed several more, including two in which I sealed up twenty-five pounds of rice. I also bought some old screw-top jars in which I packed five pounds of salt.

I was now getting near the end of my food list, though I had still not bought my tea. Making a cup of tea just before sundown at the end of a day's work had been a ritual of mine for years, but I reluctantly decided to limit myself to two pounds. So often in the past I had kept tea too long until it went fusty. It would be a waste of money to take a larger stock, though the very day I took the tea back to my room I repacked it in small containers—any tins I could find, such as baking-powder tins with press-top lids, which I filled right up to the top so there would be virtually no air space, and then sealed each lid with a rim of sticking plaster.

For a similar reason, I only bought four one-pound tins of butter. However carefully it is packed, butter invariably goes rancid after a time.

Tobacco was a real luxury. I don't smoke a great deal, but one cigarette has always seemed to go with that evening cup of tea I love so much. I bought half a pound of tobacco and a dozen packets of cigarette papers.

At first I was unable to decide whether or not to take a shotgun. I had heard rumours that the coast-watchers had left some pigs on the island, which would be quite wild by now, perhaps savage. And, too, I knew there were plenty of birds on Suvarov. But there were several reasons against taking a gun. I don't *like* killing living things; nor could I really afford a gun. But perhaps the deciding factor was that I was afraid of becoming dependent on a weapon which would be valueless when the last cartridge had been fired. I felt I had to meet the challenge of Suvarov on terms which would not change with the years. For the same reason I refused to take a small battery-operated radio. I imagine that subconsciously I was afraid I would miss its company after the batteries had run down.

By now there was very little else I needed. I bought a few odds and ends—a tin of pepper, a couple of jars of curry powder (to flavour food when all else failed), a dozen large bars of laundry soap, a dozen cakes of toilet soap.

I packed all the food in wooden boxes or cartons I had been collecting—I am *always* collecting things—lining each box with newspapers or magazines, which I knew would come in useful for all sorts of things, including lining shelves, when I reached Suvarov.

During the last week, more farewell gifts arrived. I

had never realised how many friends I had. One presented me with a twenty-five-pound tin of malted milk powder. Another gave me a twenty-five-foot bamboo fishing pole—it was rare in Rarotonga to find one quite so long—which I added to several saplings I had cut for making fishing spears, just in case I could not find any straight ones on the island.

Those stalwart friends of the P.W.D. lent me a pick and shovel; a storekeeper gave me a kerosene case which was made to hold two square four-gallon kerosene tins. The two empty tins were thrown in with the case. I cut the tops off each tin and then packed them both, and the odd spaces around them, with some of my smaller belongings. I knew that once I reached the island the tins would be invaluable for boiling clothes.

I even managed to swap a shirt for a crowbar which I considered a vital necessity. It was, in fact, the transmission shaft of an old model "T" Ford, which I took to a blacksmith who sharpened one end to a point and the other to a chisel edge.

My money—to say nothing of time—was running out, yet there were several tools I badly needed, despite the fact that I had accumulated quite an assortment over the years including chisels, a hacksaw and carpenters' saws, an axe and tomahawk, a couple of machetes, a sheath knife, as well as pliers, an adjustable spanner, and things like a hammer, screwdriver and a rat-tail file.

All the same, I required a few more items, which I bought during the last week. I needed a couple of really good chisels for I expected to find empty fuel drums left by the watchers. I bought a pair of tin-snips in case the tin roof of the shack should need attention. And when I was in the hardware store, it suddenly seemed a wise precaution to buy two tins of paint to protect any new building I might have to erect. I needed some spare hacksaw blades and when I bought some eighteen-inch lengths of round iron, with the idea of making them into spears, I had to buy two extra files. I had made enough fish spears in the past to know that even the toughest file doesn't last for ever. Then I bought a selection of nails, a hundred assorted fishing hooks and a spare hank of fishing line. Lastly I bought a small vice, which I would need if ever I had to heat and shape metal.

While accumulating all this gear, I was also busy buying seeds for the garden I knew I would have to make. I bought packets of tomatoes, cucumbers, rock melon (known in Europe as canteloupes), water melon, runner beans and Indian spinach, which trails along the ground with thicker, fleshier leaves than ordinary spinach.

I also purchased some shallots, a few tubers of sweet potatoes or yams—known in the Cooks as kumeras, an old Maori word—which I knew would quickly send up shoots which could be pulled out and planted. Finally, I bought two banana shoots in case the banana trees on the island had been torn down by a hurricane.

By now, my tiny shack was jammed to the ceiling with crates and parcels, and I had barely enough room to turn around when I made myself a cup of tea. Yet the shopping was not quite ended, for I still had to buy one or two things for my kai room. I had very nearly all I needed, for my belongings accumulated over the years included everything—crockery, cutlery, glasses, tin-openers (I never travelled without two) enamel and zinc bowls, a hurricane lantern and a glass table lamp, even a coffee-grinder as well as a coffee-pot, dishcloths and tea-towels and, above all, my old silver teapot which I had used since I left the Navy.

In addition, I had about a dozen square one-gallon screw-top glass jars which fitted into their original case.

Shopping List for a Desert Island

I had bought them about a year before with Suvarov in the back of my mind. They would be invaluable for storing the food I had bought in bulk; however, I did not plan to fill them before we reached the island in case they got broken on the voyage.

I bought several more articles for the kai room. Firstly, I decided to invest a precious £2 10s. on a six-pint cast-iron kettle, which would not deteriorate in the same way as aluminium when used over an open fire.

I also bought a big square of kitchen linoleum for the table. Throughout my "batching" days I had always insisted, even when alone, on eating off a table cloth, but for the island I thought washable linoleum would be simpler.

Otherwise, the rest of my kitchen purchases were fairly simple—plenty of spare wicks for the lantern and lamp, twelve dozen boxes of matches and four five-gallon tins of kerosene.

And now I gave some thought to the "home-front." I decided it was imperative to take a cat, for though I knew Suvarov had virtually no insects or mosquitoes, it did have a colony of small indigenous rats. With all my carefully sealed tins, it was unlikely they would eat me out of shack and home, but I just happen to hate rats. As I was already the possessor of an old cat with a kitten I decided to take them both with me, and so that they should travel in style I built a special box to house them for the six-day boat journey.

We were not old friends. As a matter of fact, I had only had the mother cat for a very short time, and she was a confirmed thief which seemed a good reason for calling her Mrs. Thievery. The son I named Mr. Tom-Tom.

Only one thing more was necessary to make me completely self-sufficient, and this was a dozen large, volcanic stones—beyond price, but without any financial value. I dug them out of a creek bed not far from where I lived and carried most of them back to my room—which was now beginning to look like a warehouse—one at a time on the saddle of my bicycle.

Each one of these large stones weighed between eight and twelve pounds. I knew stones like this just couldn't be found on Suvarov and I needed these heat-resisting stones to make a native oven. Coral is no use, for it crumbles after being used only once or twice.

With the last of my money I now went in search of my greatest luxury—a few books. Two days before the sailing date, I spent a morning browsing among the paperbacks on sale along Main Road. I had a few books already by Defoe, Stevenson and other favourite authors. Frisbie's *Island of Desire* was certainly amongst them, but when it came to spending my last few shillings on reading matter, my choice was dictated by the stocks I could inspect. I knew that the coast-watchers had left some books on the island, but I had no certainty that they would please my taste. I *had* to take a few of my own choice—not many, for I derive great pleasure from re-reading the same book (so long as I like it), but I was able to pick up three books by Somerset Maugham, two by Dickens (including *Oliver Twist*), *Mutiny on the Bounty* by Nordhoff and Hall (whom I had met on occasion), and several rather poor quality Westerns and Edgar Wallace thrillers which featured predominantly on the local bookshelves.

On the last night but one, when I was riding my bicycle to the friend who had promised to keep it for me, I stopped by a small general store and picked up a book which was to give me great pleasure in the months ahead. Indeed, I must have read it a score of times. It was a dog-eared, second-hand copy of *Lord Jim*.

With this treasure clutched under my arm, I cycled to the house where I was to "park" my bicycle. I was just about to set off on the walk home when, for some ridiculous reason, I took the pump off the crossbar.

"What on earth do you need that for?" My friend must have thought me crazy.

I couldn't answer. I just felt that I must take *everything*—just in case it came in useful.

Somehow or other, everything was ready in time. In all, I had twenty-one packages, twelve stones, two cats and my bamboo pole and saplings—plus a bundle of long-handled tools and a broom.

The *Mahurangi* was due to sail for Palmerston Island on the evening of August 29. That same morning I gathered all my gear together and Dick Brown sent up his lorry to collect it—and me. Having arrived at the wharf, it took us some hours to stow away all this cargo, since I insisted on watching every single bundle as it was stacked away in the after-hold. Had one of these parcels vanished, it could have made all the difference to my life on Suvarov.

The moment had almost arrived. I was leaving Rarotonga perhaps for ever. It gave me a queer sensation and I remember thinking, "Neale, remember you owe the P.W.D. a pick and shovel." On that last day, Rarotonga—which I had disliked so much because of the work which chained me—suddenly seemed much more attractive than ever before, and the strip of dusty Main Road which separated the lagoon from the shops seemed alive with acquaintances stopping to shake my hand and wish me luck, and there is no doubt that there was an element of sadness behind my confidence.

These were very natural thoughts, but inside I was calm in the certainty that I was doing the right thing. Even more reassuring was a profound belief that I could make a go of it. I was equipped down to the last copper nail, so far as my budget would allow. I had forgotten nothing. All that remained was for me to say good-bye to the friends I had made in the frustrating years spent in and around Rarotonga.

This I did on the last afternoon, after I had watched the final cases being packed in to the *Mahurangi*.

And then, not four hours before sailing time, everything went wrong. At a moment's notice, the sailing plans were changed. Horrified, I learned that instead of calling at Palmerston the *Mahurangi*'s orders were to sail directly to Manihiki on a new route which would pass nowhere near Suvarov.

For a time I was unable to believe the news. I almost ran all the way down to the wharf to find Dick. Everything I owned in the world—excepting my bicycle—was on board. I had vacated my room; I had nowhere to sleep, nothing to sleep on, no clothes to wear, no food to eat and no money to buy food.

"You can't do this!" My voice must have echoed my desperation.

"I'm awfully sorry, Tom—" Dick really *did* look sorry—"but the Palmerston Island trip is postponed until we return from Manihiki."

He was very kind, assuring me it wouldn't be long before my chance would come again. But at that moment I could have cried, even though I knew this sort of thing was always happening on the inter-island trading boats. Life in the South Seas does not know the same tempo as big ports and cities; a few weeks' delay rarely matters to the island folk brought up in a different tradition. Should they find themselves in my situation, as likely as not relatives or friends will put them up for a week or two, for life is not only easy but cheap.

Many a time in the past, when I was working on the

schooners, our sailing directions had been changed at the last moment. But that had been different.

As I stood there on the wharf wondering dully what would happen now, one thought was uppermost—I was virtually penniless. What was I going to do during the period of waiting? It must have been with a sense of desperation that I dived my hand into the pocket of my khaki shorts, and brought out some small change.

"Look—" I showed it to Dick—"that's all the money I have in the world."

And it was. The loose coins added up to five shillings and eightpence, for I had deliberately spent all my money before sailing as money would have no value on Suvarov. It struck me that what had happened now merely illustrated one of the reasons I wanted to get away.

After my first anger had subsided, I found I couldn't honestly blame Dick. I just had to pull myself together and face up to the situation.

I turned to him again.

"It's all I've got," I said. "Lend me ten pounds and I'll pay you back when I come back from Suvarov— if I ever do."

Dick was the sort of man who always carried a fair amount of money in his pocket. Without demur, he handed me two five-pound notes.

I was able to off-load my belongings before the *Mahurangi* sailed . . . all except the stones and three big cases buried beneath other cargo. Fortunately, I had kept lists of the contents of each package. Dick's lorry took eighteen of them back to the room after I had arranged to rent it again for a few weeks longer.

Before the *Mahurangi* sailed, I went to the skipper and every member of the crew, begging them to look after the three cases I could not off-load. And my stones! Oven stones were precious and those boys on Manihiki were bound to pinch them if they had half a chance.

But though my precious stones and cases returned safely, it took over another month before I finally did sail on October 1. We reached Suvarov on October 7, 1952.

Part Two

ON THE ISLAND

October 1952 - June 1954

3. *The First Day*

It was 1.30 p.m. as we chugged slowly towards the pass. I stood leaning over the gunwale, sipping from a tin of warm beer, watching Frisbie's "island of desire" —which was now about to become *my* island—as we prepared to drop anchor a hundred yards off shore. This was an experience I did not want to share with anyone.

The journey northwards had been uneventful. I knew several of the crew—good-hearted, cheerful, bare-chested boys from the outer islands in search of adventure—and we carried nine native passengers as well as myself. There were five women and four men, all returning to Manihiki after visiting relatives in Raro, and they were bursting with the infectious exuberance of people just ending a wonderful holiday in the "big city." The forward deck was cluttered with their farewell gifts; everything from newly-plaited hats to bundles of protesting chickens. Like all holidaymakers, they were taking home things they could just as easily have bought on their own island, but these were invested with all the importance of souvenirs or gifts.

They were a jolly crowd, but something had made me keep to myself for most of the trip. One might have thought I would eagerly seize the opportunity of sharing these last few days in the company of my fellow men, but in fact the opposite happened. Perhaps I was too excited; perhaps I was a little afraid.

As the captain—eyes fixed on the two rocks marking the channel—bellowed orders, I stood a little apart from the others, filled with a tremendous excitement surging up inside me. But I have never been a demonstrative man and I doubt whether the crew or passengers crowding the rails had the slightest inkling that this was a moment so remarkable to me that I could hardly believe it was really happening.

The sun beat down harshly; scarcely a ripple disturbed the lagoon as we edged our way through the pass, and the white beach, which I had last seen with Andy from the cabin top of the *Tiare Taporo*, came closer and closer.

My landing was hardly spectacular. Not far off the old wrecked pier the crew lowered a ship's boat and loaded my belongings aboard, and rowed me ashore. As the *Mahurangi*'s skipper had decided to stay in the lagoon until the following morning, my boat was followed by the passengers anxious for the chance to stretch their legs. So I came ashore in crowded company and almost before my crates and stores had been off-loaded, the beach was busy with women washing clothes whilst the men hurried off to fish.

Quite suddenly, though still in the company of human beings, I felt a momentary pang of loneliness. Everybody seemed so busy that nobody had any time to notice me. The crew was already rowing back to the *Mahurangi*, the laughing, brown women were sorting out their washing, the fishermen had disappeared, while I stood, feeling a little forlorn, on the hot white beach under a blazing sun, surrounded by a mound of crates, parcels, and black stones, unceremoniously dumped near the pier. A plaintive miaow reminded me I had a friend. Mrs. Thievery was impatiently demanding her freedom. Leaving all my packages on the beach, except my

The First Day

Gladstone and the box with the cats, I walked almost apprehensively the fifty yards up the coral path to the shack.

I was in some way reluctant to get there, wondering what I would find. Was it still going to be habitable? Were the water tanks still in good order? All sorts of anxieties crowded into my mind. Was there anything left of the garden which the coast-watchers had started, and what about the fowls they had left behind? Then there was the old boat. I had seen no sign of it on the beach.

I quickened my step along the narrow path, brushing past the tangled undergrowth and creepers, the dense thickets of young coconuts, pandanus, gardenias, which had grown into a curtain, walling me in, almost blocking out the sun.

Suddenly the shack was there in front of me and I must admit my heart sank. I had forgotten the amazing violence of tropical growth; forgotten, too, just how long ago it was since men had lived here. Subconsciously, I had always remembered Suvarov when the shack had been inhabited. And now, standing there with my bag and box at my feet, I could hardly distinguish the galvanised iron roof through the thick, lush creepers covering it. The outbuildings, too, seemed almost strangled beneath a profusion of growth. Cautiously I stepped on to the veranda which ran the length of the shack. The floorboards felt firm, but when I looked up at the roof, I saw the plaited coconut fronds had rotted away. And then, at one end of the veranda I spotted the boat, upside down—with two quarter-inch cracks running right along her bottom. I knew immediately she would sink like a stone in the water; nor was this realisation made any less depressing by the knowledge I had brought no caulking with me.

It was all rather overpowering. I sat in the hot sun, mopped my brow and opened up my faithful Gladstone bag and took out the screwdriver which I had packed on top of my clothes in order to be able to unscrew the netted top of the box and release the cats. In a moment the mother had jumped out, looking around her, and I set the kitten down alongside. Unlike me, they did not seem a bit deterred and proceeded to make themselves at home immediately. Within five minutes Mrs. Thievery had killed her first island rat.

I rolled myself a cigarette, sat on the veranda for a few moments and looked around at the scene I remembered so well from my one brief visit.

The end of the veranda—which was about seven feet wide—had been walled in to make an extra room, which the coast-watchers had used as their kai room. In front of the shack the ground had been cleared to form a yard which was in hopeless confusion, with weeds and vines trailing across it, dead coconut fronds blown in on stormy nights littering every corner.

At the end of the yard was a storage shed and bathhouse, also overgrown with vines, while to my left were the remnants of the garden. After one glance at the tangled wreckage of its fence I turned away. Time enough later for these problems. First I must look over the shack. So, getting up, I pushed open my front door.

Oddly, this act gave me a curious sensation, an almost spooky feeling as though I were venturing across the threshold of an empty, derelict building which held associations I couldn't know anything about. As though, in fact, I was trespassing into someone else's past which had become lost and forgotten, but was still somehow personal because the men who had lived here must have left some vestige of their personalities behind.

Once I was over this, I went inside. The room was

about ten by ten. There was a high step up from the veranda and the first thing I saw was a good solid table up against the wall facing me. Nearby was a home-made kitchen chair.

High on the wall to my left I saw two shelves holding some fifty paperback books. Two of the walls had been pierced for shutters and I opened them to let in air and light. These were typical island shutters, hinged at the top, opening upwards and designed to be kept open with a pole.

This had been the radio room, and it would make an excellent office, I thought; a sort of writing room where I could keep my few papers and, each evening, record the day's events in my journal. And the barometer would look very handsome nailed to the wall over the table. Indeed, when I took down one or two books and riffled their pages, it did not need much imagination on my part to invest the roughly hewn table with the more dignified title of desk and visualise the small, square room not so much as four rather bare walls, but as my study.

A footstep outside interrupted my daydream, and as I turned round to see the man in the doorway, I felt a moment of irritation that even on this day I could not be left alone. But I had been unfair. It was one of the passengers, a big burly Manihiki pearl diver called Tagi, who now stood rather sheepishly, wearing nothing but a pareu, and said, "Tom, we thought you might be too busy to cook yourself a meal. When the fish is ready, come and eat with us."

Full of contrition, I accepted gratefully, for on this day of all days I had no time to cook.

"I'll give you a call when it's ready," he added cheerfully, but seemed to linger. He was filled with curiosity.

"Come in and see—not bad, eh?" I asked him.

He looked around, then followed me into the bedroom which was separated from the office by a partition five-foot high, with a narrow slip serving as a door. I opened up the other shutters. This room was double the length of the first room, and to my astonishment contained a bed. It had never entered my head that I would find a bed as for some reason I had assumed the coast-watchers would have been equipped with camp beds and I had been cheerfully resigned to sleeping on the floor until I built one. I sat down eagerly to test it. It was solidly built of wood—with no springs, I was pleased to note, for I cannot stand a bed which sags. A wooden bedside table and a small shelf, which had probably been erected to keep toilet articles on, completed the furnishings.

"I wish I had a house like this," sighed Tagi.

A practical thought now occurred to me. If the coast-watchers had left a bed, two tables, a chair and books, might they not also have left some useful articles in the kai room? I hastened to inspect it.

This room had been constructed by walling in the last third of the veranda and when I pushed open the door from the veranda and looked inside, I was astounded. In one corner was a large food safe with doors and sides of zinc netting, in another the carcass of an ancient kerosene-operated refrigerator. The fuel tank had been removed but it would still make an excellent cupboard. The hinges of the food safe seemed strong when I swung the door open and the three shelves were in good condition. To complete the furnishings, the coast-watchers had built a solid table—more of a bench, really—running nearly the length of the longest wall and facing out on to the yard, with shutters above it.

I wonder if you can appreciate the excitement I felt when I discovered this unexpected treasure. I know I had barely landed on Anchorage, yet the sight of these solid pieces of furniture—which would save me endless work—made me feel as Crusoe must have felt each time he returned to the wreck. I was so delighted that I opened the food safe and the refrigerator again for the sheer pleasure it gave me, and I remember mopping my brow and saying, "Yes, Tagi, you're right. This is a place in a million."

At the far end of this room a broken-down door led out to the cook-house, quite a decent room, roofed with flattened-out fuel drums, and walled in with slats of dried mid-rib of coconut fronds neatly nailed on to supporting poles, and giving plenty of air.

Round the back of the shack were the two water tanks, which I remembered. They were in good condition. One, built of circular corrugated iron, held about three hundred gallons; the other, a square galvanised tank, held some four hundred gallons. And when I turned on the taps excellent water came gushing out. To my relief, this was quite drinkable. The tanks must have been well built and, since they rested on a wooden platform eighteen inches above the ground, did not seem to have suffered the general process of decay. Fed from the guttering along the wall, each was almost full.

Behind the shack I discovered a latrine some eight feet deep, situated some little distance away. This handy convenience was lined with two oil drums whose bottoms had been thoughtfully knocked out. On the spur of the moment, I christened it "The House of Meditation."

As I toured my new domain, my first sensation of dismay began to evaporate in the excitement of discovering items like the food safe and the bed, and I began to think to myself that this wilderness of creepers and vines could easily be cleared up in a couple of days. Then I had another pleasant surprise—in fact, two—

after walking across the yard to take a look at the store shed and bath-house. Situated at the far end of the yard, it was shaded by parau trees which shed their hibiscus blossoms each day, so that I had to tread over a carpet of flowers to reach it.

Picking up a handful, I let them trickle through my fingers as I stood for a moment, soaking in the scene. A gap in the trees, like a window, gave me a glimpse of the lagoon, blue and still and sunlit. If I listened carefully I could hear the thunder of the barrier reef above the faint rustle of the palm fronds, until the clamour of frigate birds wheeling overhead drowned all other sounds. One more angry than the rest seemed to dive almost on to the shack, and as I watched it, I suddenly realised that the long, low building, even though covered with creepers, was solid and that Tagi had been right to envy me, for it was, in fact, going to be the best place I had ever "batched" in. I turned round to tell him, but he had gone. I had been so absorbed I had never heard him leave.

Entering the rough lean-to hut, whose walls were made of plaited coconut stretched on pandanus poles, I discovered a real treasure which the coast-watchers must have left—a coil of eight-gauge fencing wire. There were at least a hundred and fifty yards of it and it was all in excellent condition.

Jutting off the shed was the bath-house, with a water tank on a stand, and a half-wall of flattened tin drums. It was badly overgrown with creepers but it would be easy to hack these down, and in no time I would be able to build a shelf for my washbowl, and put up a line for my towels.

I was on the point of leaving the bath-house when I got a real start. An old hen, clucking with fear, rose right up under my feet and made off into the bush. I had a comfortable feeling that eggs might be available in future.

Now I took a look at the garden, or rather the remains of the garden, overgrown with weeds and thick creepers. Once there had been a fence, but now only a few poles stuck out like rotten teeth, adorned with once-taut wire whose remnants lay tangled on the ground. One glance told me that whatever topsoil there might once have been had long since blown away. Right away it was obvious that re-making the garden was going to be a major problem. Only a single breadfruit tree in one corner of the wilderness gave a hint that the soil was at least fruitful.

I had been so preoccupied in exploring my new home that I only became aware of how hungry I was when Tagi returned to summon me down to the meal on the beach. But later, as we sat there against a background of palms with the lagoon stretching away in front of us and the *Mahurangi* riding at anchor a hundred yards out, I couldn't help watching my companions' faces and wondering what they would be doing at this time the following day, the following week, the following month, the following year. Would they remember this meal—and this lonely character who had chosen to stay behind on the island? Would they ever remember me at all once they had sailed away in the schooner?

It was an odd sensation. But somehow I did not very much care whether they chose to remember or not. For now I was quite sure I had broken free, though it was hard, sitting there eating fish with my fingers, to search inside myself for words which described what it felt like.

They might not remember me, but, I wondered, would I ever remember them? How, in later years, would I look back on this last meal? I overtly watched the five women who had finished their washing (which was laid on the beach, weighted down at each corner with lumps of coral) as they feasted, without a care in the world. Jolly, handsome-looking women, mostly inclined to plumpness from eating too much poi, they grabbed whatever they could—from the tasty fish and crays to the ugly over-rich coconut crabs. We all ate off banana or breadfruit leaves, while a kettle boiled noisily on the small fire, and there was a great deal of laughter and giggling and suddenly I found myself being envious of *them*. The Cook Islanders are such happy-go-lucky people, untouched by the onslaught of tourism, tha nobody can help liking them. They were contented, no doubt about that, and they didn't have to *search* for happiness. They were simpler than we whites in the South Seas, they took their pleasures as they came. I was the odd fish at that fishy meal!

Once we had finished, there was still plenty of daylight and Tagi announced that the men would carry my packages up to the shack.

No sooner had they started, however, than the five women also surged towards the yard. Now that I had shared their meal, they felt they had earned the right to see where I was going to live, to satisfy a curiosity that I found rather touching because of its innocence.

I couldn't be angry, for these weren't predatory females anxious to probe the secrets of a crank. They accepted me for what I was, and wanted to see if I would be comfortable.

They obviously thought I was *not* going to be comfortable, for when they had gathered in the yard, a great deal of gesticulating accompanied a torrent of words.

In a way, I was anxious to get down to work for I had all my belongings to sort out.

"What's the row about?" I asked, a little crossly.

"The women say your veranda roof is no good," replied Tagi.

"I could have told you that," I retorted.

"They would like to make a new one," he added.

And they did! Almost before the last of my packages had been deposited in the shack, five giggling women were squatting on my veranda burdened with fronds. They worked to such good effect that over half a new roof had been finished before the *Mahurangi* sailed the following morning.

I had little time that first evening to explore my island. Indeed, all I could do was unpack the few necessities I required, for as I wrote on the first page of my journal, "Haven't had time for a proper look around, but I can see miles of work sticking out. There will be no time for sitting under a tree and watching the reef, not for a long time anyway."

Soon after sundown, after I had entered this in my journal, I rolled a last cigarette before turning in. I was either too tired or maybe too excited even to brew a pot of tea.

I had unpacked a little glass and crockery and now I used some of my precious soap to scrub down my eating table. I put a couple of drinking coconuts on the shelf near the bed and then I unrolled my kapok mattress, spread it out and made my bed carefully.

I had had no time to examine the books left by the coast-watchers, but in any event it did not matter, for on this first night only one book seemed appropriate. When the cats had settled down, I lit the glass table lamp, carried it to the bedside table, and soon I was tucked in reading *The Island of Desire*.

Only once did I wake during the night, when a sudden squeal, half human, half animal, made me jump up, frozen with fear. It was succeeded by a series of grunts—

and then I knew the sounds and relaxed. It seemed that the rumours I had heard of wild pigs on the island were true.

The *Mahurangi* sailed soon after dawn. Over the years I had imagined this moment dozens of times, often wondering what sort of emotions I would experience at the actual moment of severing my last contact with the outside world. I had imagined I might be a little despondent and had thought, too, there might be a sudden surge of almost frightening loneliness. But now the schooner was leaving I felt nothing but impatience that the ship took so long to get under way.

I hate protracted farewells at the best of times, and yet I would have been abnormal had I not felt a pang or two of emotion. It was not despondency. It was not fear. But when Tagi, who was the last to get into the ship's boat came and said, "Best of luck, Tom!", I will admit there was a lump in my throat. It was the severing of the link, the rather ceremonious way he shook hands, that made me feel that way; but it passed quickly.

At last all the passengers were on board, and the old *Mahurangi* began to move. I stood on the beach watching her sail slowly towards the gap through the reef. Once she was far enough away, I took off my shorts and waved them in symbolic farewell.

From that moment onwards I never again put on those shorts. Instead, I wore a five-inch strip torn from an old pareu. I wore it native style, one end fastened round the waist, with the other end hanging down in front, then passed between the legs, drawn behind, the end being tucked under the waistband. Done properly, it will remain in position all day, whether you are working, swimming or fishing.

4. Alone at last

Now I was alone on my island I began to take stock. Since Anchorage is roughly tongue-shaped, and measures only three hundred yards at its widest point, I could take most of it in at a glance as I stood on the beach watching the *Mahurangi* disappear.

From the broken-down pier, where I had waved good-bye, I could see stretching back from the beach a profusion of coconuts, pandanus trees, vines and a mass of tauhunu—a shrub which has a habit of shooting up to twenty feet or more into an impenetrable bush. Dwarfing them all were five huge tamanu trees whose ponderous limbs jutted out from massive trunks twenty feet or more above my head. The trunks were forked and twisted like any ancient English oak, and it must have been one of these trees to which Frisbie had lashed his children during the hurricane. They certainly looked tough enough to withstand any storm.

Driven by a sudden impulse I decided that before doing anything else, I would walk right round the island, either along the beach or in the shallow waters of the fringe reef. It was not meant to be a pleasure stroll. I wanted to see something of the island, find out where the best coconuts were growing, discover the whereabouts of the best topsoil for my garden, examine the shallows with an eye to the best pools for fishing.

It was a beautiful morning, so leaving the old pier

behind me, I set off up the west coast—the lagoon side—
for the northern tip of my new home, walking at first
along a beach so white and blinding that it almost hurt
my eyes.

I hadn't gone far before I came upon a clump of coconuts shading the beach like a canopy, their slender trunks
bent by the prevailing wind so that they leaned over at an
angle of about forty-five degrees. It was not their beauty,
however, which struck me, but the more prosaic fact
that the height of the trees did not look too intimidating
for climbing. I could see there were plenty of nuts
many of them low enough to be got at with the short
pole which, in my mind, was already equipped with an
iron hook.

Behind them, the ground rose to fifteen feet, the
highest point of the island, and here the trees were taller.
Moreover, a mass of tauhunu, which thrives on sandy
atoll soil (and shares the coconut's gift for withstanding
the salt driven in from the sea), looked so thick that I
knew it would be difficult getting near many of the nuts.
There was a lot of pandanus about, too; a thin-leafed
palm looking quite different from a coconut tree, and
which Frisbhie once described as "gawky-limbed."

This was the only hill on my island, and it was not very
large, and as I walked slowly towards the northern tip,
the ground sloped down until it was barely three feet
above sea level.

At times I was able to walk along a stretch of beach but
at others the coral gave way to rock and I would paddle
through the shallows as I skirted some miniature "head-
land." It was a very clear day and along the reef
stretching north of Anchorage I could see several of the
lagoon's islets—Whale, Brushwood and One Tree Island,
with its single palm like a toy tree stuck on a piece of
cardboard placed on a sheet of glass.

Alone at last

It had taken only a few minutes to walk from the pier, half-way up the west coast, to the northern tip of the island, for the distance was hardly more than four hundred yards. Now I turned back and made my way along the white sandy beach of the east coast which stretched ahead in a series of gentle curves for half a mile to the sound end of the island. I could see no evidence of bees or insects, no reptiles; nothing more dangerous than the coconut crabs, and an occasional rat.

Some fifteen-foot miki-miki trees were growing almost out of the bare rock at the water's edge, and I made a mental note about them; I would find their hard branches invaluable, for they make the best sticks in the world for husking coconuts. A few yards farther on I spied some young paw-paws fifty yards inland and decided to give them a closer look. I had almost reached them when a violent flurry in the undergrowth scared the wits out of me. Almost before I realised what had happened, I had a glimpse of a wild pig lumbering away with astonishing speed. But my momentary fear quickly gave way to anger when I realised I had disturbed the brute in the very act of tearing out the green young shoots of some paw-paw—one of the fruits on which I would have to depend. Those pigs presented a real problem.

The rest of the paw-paws appeared to be flourishing, but nearby some old banana trees seemed to be in a sorry condition, and I could see that if I wanted any bananas I might well have to rely on the two suckers I had brought with me—and devise a means of protective fencing to keep the pigs out.

Skirting the overgrown bush, I followed the curving beach until I reached a point half-way down the east coast. Here I re-discovered a little cove, marked on the charts as Pylades Bay, where I had swum on my first visit.

This natural bathing pool was deep, and the water was blue, clear and enticing. Pylades Bay would certainly be my private swimming pool. Behind it, the ground was covered with hibiscus trees and densely matted tauhunu, and from the beach I could see several uprooted coconut trees, the long, slender, dead-straight trunks lying just where they had crashed. I remembered Frisbie telling me, "The most awesome thing in the hurricane was watching, actually watching, the wind take an old coconut tree eighty feet tall and tear it out of the ground."

These must have been the ones he had referred to when describing the hurricane of '42. I scrambled towards them, making my way past the impenetrable tauhunu along the patches of gravel here and there—some carpeted with fallen hibiscus blossoms, others bare, but covered with bird droppings, which delighted me, for I knew what that meant. This must be a nesting place for terns, which prefer to lay their eggs on bare rock in November and December. I could see the prospect of scrambled tern eggs for tea when they started to lay in three or four months' time.

The fallen coconuts were big fellows, and the way they had been strewn haphazardly made me think incongruously of a giant spilling a box of matches. They were overgrown with vines, and in some cases the roots had been torn out of the ground in their entirety.

Looking idly around, I saw a vaguely familiar object embedded in one enormous, spreading, upturned root, and with some difficulty I managed to dislodge it. It was a brick, apparently made from fire clay and in perfect condition. As far as I could see, it had never been used, and must have lain buried under the coconut palm for fifty years or more. No doubt it had been left there from the days when Lever Brothers were growing copra on the island. I tucked it under my arm, for everything can have a use on an uninhabited island.

The southern part of the island had obviously fared worst in the hurricane, and I had only to look around me to see the reason why, for though the northern end was protected by the barrier reef, the gigantic waves which had poured through the pass must have hit the south end of the island with their full force, so that near the southern tip a depression sliced its way across the island where heavy seas had swept right over Anchorage. This savage onslaught had done some good, however, for it was here that I now discovered a large amount of topsoil. Picking up a handful, I felt its gritty, fine sand and knew it was exactly what I wanted—though at this stage I did not even contemplate how I would transport it to the garden, a quarter of a mile away.

The day was so clear that looking across the lagoon I could even see Motu Tuo, where Andy and I had picnicked, and I remember on that first warm morning that hardly a breeze was stirring the coloured patchwork of the lagoon. And I can remember, too, standing ankle-deep in the shallows, looking at my own palm-tree skyline of Suvarov and saying to myself, "Well, Neale, here you are after all these years—*and it's all yours.*"

During the next few days I was so busy getting straight that I never seemed to have time to cook or even think about meals. But this didn't worry me because I knew a more settled time was coming when I had established a routine. And meantime I just seemed to sink naturally into this new island life. After all, I had had more than half a lifetime of preparation. My succession of jobs in the engine rooms of a dozen different island vessels had taught me how to handle tools. Indeed, I was used to coping with any practical problem that turned up, whilst my jobs on shore—clearing bush, planting bananas, even storekeeping—had taught me the hard way of fending for myself. I *was* the handyman incarnate. I knew four different ways to thatch a roof; I could spear fish; I was able to light a fire with a magnifying glass—not that I ever needed this trick for by now I knew exactly the kind of wood which smouldered but never burst into flame, so that I was able to keep a fire dormant all through the night.

I was immensely happy during those first few days. Before starting to unpack everything, I cleaned out the shack thoroughly, scrubbing the floors and washing down the walls. Then I spent three or four days hard at work tearing down the creepers and vines from the roof of the shack and hacking them away from the shed with my machete. I finished plaiting the veranda roof and had to nail up two of the shutters which had become loose. There seemed no end to the work, but before long I had made a shelf in the bath-house and then I fixed up a clothes line between two hibiscus trees at the bottom of the yard, and high enough to hang out my bed linen.

All this took a long time for I had to fish for the cats (and myself!) and though I did very little cooking at first, I had to make a fire and this meant collecting firewood from all over the island. But I was determined to clean up the place before I did anything else, and only when this was done did I set about sorting out my supplies.

One of the first tasks I had to tackle was unpacking my sack of sugar and storing the contents before it became damp in the empty screw-top jars I had brought along with me. I put these jars with the rest of my bulk food in the old refrigerator, except for the few items I knew I would need daily.

The old fridge was a real blessing for I decided my kai room was one place that must be both spotless and tidy. I suppose it is a relic of my Navy days that I like to stow things away in their proper places and keep them shipshape. One of the first things I did, just to remind me that dirty plates had no place on an idyllic island, was to fetch a length of wire and two nails and string up a line above the kai bench for my dishcloths and teacloths. I can tell you that from that moment on I always washed up in hot water and invariably kept a spare teacloth in reserve. And when I sat down to my meals I laid out my plates and cutlery—or maybe some large green leaves instead of plates—on the table linoleum I had brought for just this purpose.

From the day I unpacked, I used the top shelf of the food safe for storing the food I knew I would require daily —a jar of sugar, a tin of jam, a little tea and coffee, and so on—while on the middle shelf I kept my plates and cutlery. The bottom shelf was reserved for the small tins of cooking aids like salt, curry powder and my coffee-grinder.

I was equally meticulous about my tools. I unpacked the smaller ones—saws, chisels, hammer and so on—into a convenient box which I kept on the veranda where I could get at them easily. The bigger ones and my pick and shovel I stored in the shed in the yard, where I also had a shelf for my packages of nails, screws and bits of wire.

The cook-house did not present much of a problem, and though I dumped my volcanic stones in a corner, there was no time yet for the laborious business of making a native oven, and I contented myself at first with finding two suitably shaped stones on which to rest my bars of iron for simple cooking over an open fire. In another corner I kept a box of wooden chips and some kindling wood.

The only thing I missed was a good, wood-burning stove, like the one on which I had cooked in Moorea. They are simple to use, economical with wood, and make it much easier to keep the cookhouse tidy. I knew, almost as soon as I settled in, that this was one purchase I should have made in Rarotonga, even if it had meant sacrificing some luxury. Had there been any good volcanic stones on the island, I might have built a stone fireplace of sorts, but there were none.

Once I had unpacked, firewood was one of my top priorities, for I wanted the shed filled with a good six months' supply. In a few weeks the hurricane season would start, and that could mean a spell of heavy rainy weather. I had no intention of being caught without dry firewood.

It was a hard job. Some of the shrubs and trees had dead limbs which could be severed with a couple of strokes of the axe. But otherwise it was a business of solid, backbreaking sawing, and I relegated all other priority jobs until I had accumulated an impressive woodpile. It took me nearly two weeks to fill my shed with wood, but later, when the rainy season came, it was to prove a boon.

Kindling wood I kept separate, mainly relying on tauhunu which, when more or less rotten, would smoulder happily on my fire. I always had a couple of pieces quietly smoking on the fire in the cook-house, and found them thoroughly reliable because when I wanted to get a blaze going it was only necessary to push two smouldering ends together, pile on a few chips from the box I kept handy, and in no time at all there would be a splendid blaze going. Indeed, this system worked so well that it was very seldom that I had to use a match, and as time went by it became almost a point of honour never to have to reach for the box.

Almost without noticing it, I slipped into the routine that was to become my life. Early morning had a familiar sound for I was regularly awakened by a rooster just before dawn. I would lie there relaxed for a little, thinking how lucky I was to look forward to a day which was going to bring me nothing but satisfaction. And then, as it grew light, I would get up and fill the cast-iron kettle and light a fire. Usually the embers were still warm. Once the kettle was on and the fire going, I invariably made for the "House of Meditation" for I have always been a creature of regular habits.

Close at hand was an old tin with the top cut off. Filled with ashes, it served as a practical alternative to modern plumbing.

Then off I went for a quick wash before breakfast; only a cat's lick since I reserved my "shower" for the end of the day after hard work in the hot sun.

Back in the kai room the kettle would be boiling and the cats impatient for their fish (which I had saved from the night before). And whilst they ate I would get down a pound jar of coffee which I had ground from my supply of beans and brew myself a couple of cups to accompany a Suva biscuit or two, with butter and jam—though later, when I was more settled, I baked scones and, later still, would often have eggs for breakfast.

I rarely ate a substantial lunch. During those first months there was so much to do that I could not bear to waste time on cooking until the evening. I could easily find drinking nuts, and if I felt a pang of hunger around midday, I would chew some uto—the inside of a young sprouting coconut, which can be eaten either cooked or raw. (I shall have more to say about uto later on.)

77

My dislike of cooking (only because it wasted time) amounted almost to a phobia at first, because I could not really adjust myself to the tempo of this new life, to the fact that I did not really need to hurry. Instinctively I wanted to get any job done as quickly as possible, and at times I would be spurred on by melancholy thoughts that I would never get my garden started or build a run and raise the fowl population.

After work, I would catch some fish in the early evening, cook it and then, if the weather were fine, take a bowl of tea down to the beach and sit there on a box-chair which I had made so I could watch the sun go down—one of my favourite "pastimes."

Then I would "explore" something very different from my daytime activities—the books left by the coast-watchers. These were a mixed bag, I must admit, and if I describe my own taste in literature as catholic, I don't know what denomination to use in describing theirs!

I decided that half of them were not worth reading at all—a decision I reversed after a year when I was only too glad to read *anything*. But there were some gems among the trash, including several books of which I had never heard.

One evening I picked up *Brave New World* by Aldous Huxley. I remember I was very tired that night, and meant to read only a few pages to lull me to sleep. I was kept awake half the night, entranced by a description of a world so horrifying that time after time I would stop, reflect on what I had read, and say, "Neale —if *that*'s what the world is going to be like, you just stay where you are!" Even the crowing of a cock could not have wakened me that morning!

During the first weeks the problems of settling in occupied most of my time, but I did make a tentative start on some of the more long-term projects I had in mind.

Though the prospect of eggs for breakfast seemed remote, I tried to cajole the fowls by scattering grated coconut at the far end of the yard. I had plans to tame them and collect them all into one run and after the first couple of weeks I noticed they were a lot less hesitant about approaching the shack.

Unfortunately, my gifts of grated coconut also attracted the wild pigs; five large and destructive animals whose feverish passion for uprooting everything in sight made me acutely conscious that my plans for a garden were not likely to come to fruition with these menaces about.

Nonetheless, the garden was a necessity. What was left of it was about forty feet long, and eventually I knew I would have to fence it in. But since I certainly could not cope with this task just then, I contented myself meantime with trying to preserve the breadfruit tree which stood near the cook-house. I managed this by sawing off four equal lengths of coconut log from some fallen trees and with them I constructed a sort of frame around its roots. Every day after this I tipped in a mixture of old leaves and scraps of food, fish the cats had left and even fishbones, all stirred up to make humus which would nourish the roots and ensure me a regular and invaluable supply of breadfruit for my table.

At one end of what was left of the garden I planted the two banana suckers I had brought. Although I tended them in just the same way, there was a year to wait before I enjoyed my first bunch of bananas. Once the trees had started, however, they never looked back.

I managed to fit in these jobs between my daily routine and I was lucky in that the weather contrived to remain almost perfect during those first few weeks, So much so that the first month went past so rapidly I could hardly believe it when I came to enter up my diary for November 6, and discovered this was my birthday. I see from my journal that I noted this Friday "a beautiful warm day, the breadfruit tree is doing fine. Took my tea down to the beach after catching fish for the cats. Cooked them on the beach just before dusk and watched the night fall on the lagoon." And then, because the date took me back into an existence I had half forgotten, I found myself adding, "Fifty-one years ago today my mother was having a tough time."

I found it difficult to believe I had actually spent a whole month on the island. Does this sound impossible? Believe me, it did not seem so to me. Every day had been so full, what with my simple endeavours to get my roots down and establish myself on the island, that the time just seemed to have disappeared and I was sometimes so busy I would even forget my resolution to shave every Wednesday and Sunday, or boil my bed linen once a week.

And now here I was in November with the hurricane season due any moment, so that suddenly I had to turn-to and get down to definite measures which would ensure my survival.

Since the shack was my home, its preservation became my first thought. I knew I had to evolve a scheme which was going to make it stand up to whatever the winds could do, so I decided to peg it down with guy ropes made from the wire left by the coast-watchers.

I started by digging three holes on each side of the shack, holes designed to anchor the wire I planned to rig right over the roof. The next thing was to make good strong "anchors" for the guy ropes as any normal method of pegging would never stand up to a big wind.

For each of the six holes I had dug, I dragged up fifty-pound squarish lumps of coral, dumped them on the edge and wound them round and round with wire, leaving a big loop of wire sticking out from each one.

Then I lowered the stones into the holes, and filled them up so that only the loops remained above ground. Next I cut three long lengths of wire off the roll and slung them right over the roof of the shack. All I had to do now was fasten the two ends of each length through the loops on either side of the shack and tighten the wires by twisting them with my pliers.

This major job took me quite a few days but when it was completed I felt much more secure—though I didn't flatter myself that my efforts would outlast a hurricane of the calibre of '42. But for ordinary storms, I reckoned I could hold my own.

There was one final precaution: I dug a hole about five feet long and three feet wide in the shed to hold my survival kit which consisted of my box of tools, to which I added three boxes of matches in a tin sealed with sticking plaster and a spare pair of rubber shoes. And from now on I practised a "drill." Whenever my barometer indicated a severe storm coming up, my box went straight into that hole. Without it, I knew there was little chance of my survival.

5. Fishing, Cooking—and Improvising

MIRACULOUSLY, the storms left us alone. There were sudden squalls which blotted out everything five yards from the shack but these were shortlived and indeed were welcome, for they not only cooled the island but replenished my water tanks. I did not count them as "bad weather," however, and during the first autumn there were no signs of the hurricanes I had feared.

It was just as well, for during the next few months I began to work harder than I had ever done before in my life. And yet this was something I never resented because everything that cropped up seemed to come as a challenge and every time I managed to find the answer, it was a new step forward that seemed tremendously worthwhile.

Often after a hard day I would imagine myself back in Rarotonga, where I might have been waiting impatiently for Friday's pay-packet. But here mundane things like that had no significance. Instead, I would relax in the evening and, if the weather were fine, I would brew myself a bowl of tea and carry it down to the beach. There I would sit with the faint sigh of the trade winds rustling the palms which bent like a canopy over my head. Sometimes I would light a small fire to cook the cats' supper, and later Mr. Tom-Tom or Mrs. Thievery would jump up on my lap and purr contentedly.

On some evenings the air would be so still I could hear my own breath; at others, my little world would be filled with the screams and sounds of birds wheeling above me, mostly the terns (which I watched patiently, for I knew they would soon start to lay) and frigate birds, which nested on the islets in their thousands, knowing they had no humans to fear. I never ceased to be fascinated by these ugly brutes, with a wing span of up to eight feet and scarlet pouches below their bills. They are born bullies. Four or five would start chasing one poor little tern until they had forced it to disgorge the fish it had just caught, and then, with an incredible dexterity on the wing, would invariably catch the fish before it struck the water.

At least they provided drama during those moments between day and night—made all the more inviting by the absence of mosquitoes or flies.

Night fell around us with startling tropical swiftness, so that one moment the lagoon would resemble a patchwork quilt of colours and the next would become a black satin bedspread—yes, that is what it looked like, a giant's bedspread, with the white foam of the reef like the tops of the sheets and pillows.

I was entirely content. Nothing could seem more perfect, and as the embers of my fire died down, the cats came closer to me, as though reminding me that this particular day was over, and now it was time to sleep and gather strength for the new day ahead.

And when the new day dawned, there were always two vital necessities which seemed to dominate every other plan I had in mind. They were fishing and cooking and it did not take me long to discover the most likely spots where my staple food was waiting to be hooked or speared, for the pools in the shallows along the reef abounded (and I use that overworked word deliberately) in all kinds of fish. It was only a question of choosing between the small ku, parrot fish, eels, cod or crayfish.

Nor was I worried by sharks, barracuda or other dangerous fish, which rarely penetrated as far as these shallow
waters (though I did have two encounters with sharks
later on).

One of the simplest fish to catch—and one of the tastiest
—were cray, on the barrier reef at night on a rising tide.
Often I could see their feelers sticking out of a crevice,
and since a cray invariably faces outwards from the hole
in which it hides, I was able to catch hold of the feelers
with my right hand, slide my left into the crevice, grab
him and start pulling. The cray is quite difficult to
dislodge and I had to keep up a steady strain. Once he
tired, however, it was easy, When I got him out, I
would give the tail a quick twist to kill him.

Quite by chance, I discovered a crayfish "reservoir."
Walking along the reef one morning I came on a pool
about eighteen inches deep with a white coral lining
showing clearly through the water. At that very moment
a cray scuttled like a flash from one crevice to another.

I thought I had spotted where it had taken refuge and
poked after it with the shaft of my spear. For a few
moments nothing happened and I supposed I had stuck
the shaft into the wrong crevice, but just as I was about
to pull the spear out, I felt a curious vibration in my hand.

And that meant a cray was hiding in the hole, for long
ago in Moorea I had learned from the native fishermen
that if you happen to touch a hidden cray a vibration
travels up the pole. The cray doesn't actually move—
at least, I don't think it does; it must be the fishy
equivalent of a shudder of apprehension! Whatever it is,
the vibration is so marked that I could always feel it if I
were holding the spear shaft in my hand. Once I had
got this one out, I tried another crevice and sure enough
there was a vibration. I went on poking around until
the whole pool seemed alive with cray. Indeed, it proved

a fertile larder and I came back to the pool for weeks until I had exhausted the entire natural supply.

If the crayfish panicked out of sight, the parrot fish panicked in full view. Vivid blue or light reddish in colour, they lay in the small pools or depressions along the reef. Sometimes I would walk into a pool and disturb several of them—each between a foot and eighteen inches long—and then they would dart about frantically until finally, ostrich-like, they would make for some cranny in the coral and hide their heads so that I could spear their bodies easily.

The parrot is a fleshy fish from which I could usually cut a good fat fillet, and I dined on them in the early days because they taste best when eaten raw, and I was in no mood to waste time on too much cooking.

Since the days when I lived on Moorea, I had become used to eating them in the Tahitian style, raw and marinated in lime juice, but as there were no limes on Suvarov, I soaked them in a little vinegar and chopped onion which could be used over and over again.

If I did feel like cooking, then I would fish for ku, some six to nine inches long, with a delicate flavour not unlike mullet. I could easily catch half a dozen in a few minutes, using a hook which I usually baited with a feather.

I used to fry them straight away, with the heads and scales still on and once they were cooked the skin would peel off easily. Since they have a lot of bones, I seldom ate them on a plate. Instead, I used fleshy leaves from the breadfruit or paw-paw tree, which were as big as plates and obviated the necessity of washing up since I simply decanted the remnants around the roots of my breadfruit and banana trees.

My only worry when frying ku was that my supply of dripping was strictly limited, so before long I decided that

I must cook them in a native oven, a process which involved spending much more time in the cook-house, as every meal entailed building an individual oven from volcanic stones. There was just no escape from this chore because a native oven has no permanence in the sense one thinks about ovens in a civilised world. One meal—however delicious—and you've got to start rebuilding your cooking stove all over again. It's not a job I would recommend to the average housewife anxious to produce a tasty "little something" within a few minutes.

Let me tell you how I went about it. First I made a shallow hole in one corner of my cook-house, with my pile of volcanic stones handy nearby. In the hole—little more than a depression—I lit a fire, and once it was going well, ringed it with the larger stones and then carefully covered the fire by building up a sort of pyramid of the smaller stones over the burning wood, rather like putting coal on a fire started with chips. As the fire burned down to embers, the stones soon absorbed the heat so that after an hour or so the inner ones were glowing dull red. When the fire had finally burned itself out, I levelled the stones with the butt end of a palm frond and my oven was ready.

I knew the stones would retain their heat for hours and I had ready several dozen fat green leaves picked from the breadfruit tree and tied in bundles of ten. These were to form the "lid" and could be used over and over again.

Whilst the stones had been heating, I had got the fish ready, well wrapped in leaves and now I laid them on the stones gently covering them with a top layer of more clean leaves. On top of this I placed the breadfruit "lid" which I now finally covered with old mats and sacks, weighted down at the edges with stones.

Does it sound complicated? I can assure you that the result was really delicious and, what's more, I could leave my meal cooking slowly there for hours. Indeed, I would often go away on another task and return much later, confident that when I lifted the lid my dinner would be awaiting me cooked to a turn whatever time I came in.

But as the weeks went on, the actual time spent in "creating" each individual oven began to irk me. This may seem strange on a desert island where time is generally supposed to have no significance, but for me every moment lost in cooking was time wasted for more vital projects.

Yet I could cook ku no other way without losing my precious dripping. (I was secretly saving it to fry my first eggs!) Ku were too small to be boiled and they were too tender and bony to make a fish stew. How I missed a real stove! I could have kicked myself for not having brought one, but then each new week brought fresh evidence of my lack of foresight when shopping in Rarotonga. I had really believed my list was complete, that after all the experience gained during my years of batching, nothing had been left to chance; and I often reflected ruefully on the remarks of the salesman when I was buying my rubber shoes: "Let's face it, you've always been near a store."

Well, there were no stores on Suvarov and this was only one of many problems I faced, including another when I used the multiple barbed spear which a friend in Rarotonga had given me, for it tore the flesh of small fish so badly that after a few weeks of trying to eat torn and mangled fish, I decided I would have to set about constructing a single-pronged spear from one of the eighteen-inch lengths of round iron I had brought with me.

I needed an anvil to fashion my new spear and fortunately there was an old piece of ballast I had discovered on the beach which must have weighed fifty pounds.

I knew that in order to sharpen the tip I would first have to heat the iron bar over a fire, then hammer it to a point on the anvil, but only now did I realise I had never thought of buying a pair of blacksmith's tongs with which to grasp it when the heat from the tip began to creep up the bar.

To get over this, I wrapped the end I had to hold in layer after layer of the large cloth-like dead leaves which you always find attached to the base of a coconut palm frond. They are brown in colour, and very soft and pliable, and in fact look and feel rather like sacking, so they suited my purpose very well.

Once I had got a good fire going in the cook-house, I found it fairly easy to hammer the iron to a point, and when it had cooled off I filed the point down with my coarse file until it was really sharp. Then I heated it again until it was bright red, and plunged it into water several times to harden it.

After I had picked out a suitable sapling for a shaft, I cut a slot four inches deep in one end, fitted the spearhead into it, then bound the whole with wire.

Though fishing and cooking—and, I suppose, improvising—occupied a great deal of time, I had to do something about the fowls and the garden. The fowl run which I hoped to build could wait, for more and more terns were wheeling overhead by now, and I knew that it would not be long before they started to lay.

On the other hand, a garden was an absolute necessity. I could start to make a fence but my real problem lay in transporting the topsoil I had discovered by the depression at the southern end of the island.

I set off on several occasions, armed with a shovel and

a sugar sack, but it would take me an entire morning to carry one sackful to the garden. I did make a start by sifting out three sackfuls which I put into shallow boxes so that I could at least start growing seeds, though whether I would ever be able to transplant them was another matter.

My first attempts at separating the fine soil took me several days—simply because I had not thought to buy a sieve in Rarotonga. I did, however, have a small tea strainer, and I sieved enough fine soil for six seed-boxes, using only this wretchedly small implement.

How I missed a boat! I would look wistfully at the wide cracks in the upturned boat on the veranda, gaping at me as though to say, "I'll sink like a stone." Why hadn't I brought some caulking material? Then I could have mended her, hauled her through the shallows, loaded her up and pulled her back. But the boat looked impossible to repair—unless I could think of something; and I seemed to have so many other things to think about.

During this time when there was no chance of ever tasting an egg, I lived almost exclusively on fish, breadfruit, paw-paw—and uto, without doubt the most nutritious of all indigenous foods on Suvarov.

Uto is formed when a coconut has fallen from a tree and is left on the ground until it starts sprouting. At this moment nature begins a fascinating metamorphosis. Miniature coconut leaves sprout out, while inside the nut milk and meat are gradually transformed into a white spongy substance. This is uto, and you can eat it either cooked or uncooked, though over-indulgence in the latter leads to indigestion.

I discovered there was plenty of uto on the island, but

once again I ran into cooking problems. In fact, it seemed as though every time I tasted a new fruit or caught a different kind of fish, I had to devise a new way to cook it.

I started by cooking uto on a native oven, but it was unsatisfactory because you can't easily regulate the heat and overcooked uto is uneatable. I wasted so much time that I would find myself eating it raw to save the work of building the oven—and that, I knew, would in the end lead to stomach trouble.

It did. I had such a bad bout of indigestion I vowed never to eat raw uto again. But neither did I want the chore of making a native oven. I looked around for a way out, and eventually decided to try and make a special cooker for uto.

The coast-watchers had left several empty forty-gallon drums on the island. I rolled one up to the shack, and first of all cut about eighteen inches off the bottom of one so the drum resembled a giant cake tin. (It proved too tough for my tin snips and I spent two laborious days working on it with my cold chisel.) I made a hole deep enough to take the tin in a corner of the cook-house so that the top stuck out six inches or so above the ground. Next, I made a lid from the other end of the drum, though I had some difficulty as it would not fit over the top of the "cake tin" because, of course, it was exactly the same size. However, I cut slots with my hacksaw every nine inches around the edge of the lid making it just pliable enough to bend outwards a little, so that it would fit over the other section. I punched two holes in the lid and made a handle from a piece of wire.

I lit a fire inside the "cake tin" and when it was going well, threw in some volcanic stones. As soon as these grew hot, I popped in a couple of dozen husked uto nuts, with the eye-end carefully turned down—a necessity because there is little meat near the eye-end, so the uto cooks more quickly. I jammed the lid on, covered the cooker with old sacks and let the uto cook between three and four hours, timing the operation carefully. This, by the way, was virtually the only time I ever used my clock on Suvarov.

My cooker worked perfectly, and once the uto was cooked I kept it in a special box and often ate it cold with coconut cream for breakfast. It tastes remarkably like a coconut scone, and has a consistency which resembles Yorkshire pudding. It is very sustaining. If I were suddenly hungry I would go to my store, break open a cooked nut and eat the uto as one might eat an apple or a piece of cake between meals.

My basic diet, however, still continued to be fish, especially as I was hoarding my "special" supplies like a miser; I suppose instinctively I was guarding against a rainy day—literally a rainy day—when fishing might be impossible, or I could be confined to my shack.

Sometimes I would eat one of the coconut crabs which I found in small numbers on Suvarov. But I never really cared for them. They were ugly, brutal creatures, at least a foot long, with a pair of claws strong enough to crush a finger. Some of the islanders I had known considered their tails to be a great delicacy, but I found them too rich. Besides, coconut crabs are scavengers who will eat anything. They would have eaten me had I died! I roasted one occasionally when I really felt a need for a change of diet. Their claws were good, but my dislike for these repugnant creatures tended to spoil my appetite, so that when the cats and I got heartily sick of ku or rae, parrot fish, and were desperate for a change of flavour, I preferred to go after larger fish.

Trevally, a predatory fish weighing six pounds or more, prefer live bait, but having none I constructed a lure of white feathers backed up with a strip of red material from an old pareu. Quite often I would hook a trevally with the first cast from my big rod and as a great treat I would use a little dripping and have a couple of well-fried fillets for supper, though more often—especially if I caught a bigger one with coarser flesh—I would steam the head, stirring some coconut cream into the water. If cooked properly, it made a really good fish soup.

Every fish in the lagoon seemed to queue up for my table (except, curiously, turtles, which were rare). Perhaps the easiest to catch was the reef cod which lay motionless in the pools as I approached. They never even moved until my spear was within six inches of them, and once I had them quivering on shore, I carried them back to the shack and steamed them in salt water in my aluminium pan over a fire beneath a piece of flattened old iron roofing.

Both trevally and cod had to be cooked over the open fire which I kept going under my firebars resting on two lumps of coral. But more and more I was wondering how I could build myself a proper fireplace as the substitute for the stove I so sorely missed. The coastwatchers had left so much junk behind—like the fuel drums which had been so useful for making my uto cooker—that I searched everywhere in the hope of finding other things I might turn to good account. I also searched along the beach, for flotsam of one sort or another was always being washed ashore.

I collected it all. Once I found a child's ball. Empty bottles were washed up regularly, and one day I found several flat, yellowish blocks, nearly a foot square and three inches thick. As I picked up the nearest piece, I noticed some small stones partially embedded in its underside. These stones puzzled me until I realised that the substance must have softened under a hot sun and then hardened again. And then I thought of the paraffin wax my mother always used to seal the top of her jam jars. It was an odd find and in all there were half a dozen chunks of wax, weighing about twenty pounds.

This might have been of little value but nonetheless, I carried it all back to the shed in the yard—and then forgot about it, for my mind was still fixed on building a stove or fireplace.

Since the beach yielded nothing, I next turned to the fuel drums left by the coast-watchers and tried to flatten one, thinking that I might possibly build a stove out of sheet metal, but I did not have the tools. I even toyed with the idea of trying to dislodge a large slab of concrete embedded in the ground near the shack, which the coast-watchers had used as a platform for their generator—but that too proved impracticable and I left it where it was.

How infuriating to consider that one clue to building a fireplace remained right under my nose for weeks without my realising it—until one morning I went to the woodshed to get my broom which I had made out of palm fronds.

I wasn't thinking as I stepped inside the shack, and then yelled with pain as I stubbed my bare toe on a large stone. Angrily I bent down to pick it up and throw it out —and my hand grasped not a stone but the brick I had dug out of the coconut root on my first day alone on the island.

A brick! If only I had some bricks I could build the world's finest fireplace. I didn't give another thought to sweeping out my bedroom. That brick had been left by Lever Brothers fifty years ago. Why on earth would they leave just one unused brick? Might there not be some more somewhere near the spot?

Instead of the broom, I grabbed my pick and shovel,

called in at the shack for a cooked uto—which, with a drinking nut, would have to suffice for lunch—and set off to do a day's digging.

I spent five whole days—in which I abandoned every other activity but fishing—on one of my most back-breaking jobs; but my hunch was right and in the end I was rewarded by unearthing twenty-one bricks.

I knew exactly how I was going to use them, and I carried them back to my cook-house where my couple of firebars were still resting across two large stones. This was my normal cooking spot when I did not feel inclined to build a native oven; two ordinary stones which, now I had the bricks, looked so thoroughly outdated that I hurled them outside. Soon I was building a proper fireplace with a base of bricks and two sides so that I could place the firebars across them. It was neater, more serviceable and more economical than anything I had had before, and I found myself casting an almost contemptuous glance at my old friends, the volcanic stones heaped in a corner.

By December—while I was still waiting for the rains, which were unaccountably late that year—I had my first omelette since I landed on Suvarov. Thousands of terns had arrived on the island by now and the time came when they started flying around in circles, making a terrific noise. Once I saw this, I knew that they were about to start laying—and I knew, too, that those eggs would be laid in spots where there was little or no undergrowth, or even on the bare rock.

The tern is as big as a pigeon, though its black and white body is of slighter build and its food comes exclusively from the sea. Despite this, as I knew from experience, their eggs never taste fishy—in direct contrast to hens which, when fed with fish, produce very fishy-tasting eggs.

Before long, they were laying in their thousands, and terns seem to lay again and again, like fowls. Knowing their habits and being anxious to secure fresh eggs, I constructed a sort of egg trap by clearing a patch of scrub. It worked, and soon I was collecting eggs there every day. Just to make sure, I dipped them one by one into water, knowing that if the egg were fit to eat it would lie on its side at the bottom of the glass. It is an old trick. Once incubation has begun an egg will stand on end, whilst an old one can soon be spotted since it simply floats to the top.

For a month I had eggs every day, and fed the rest of my daily haul to the cats who loved them, or as sure "bait" in my gradual struggle to tame the fowls. As a matter of fact, the hens loved them, especially after I had hard-boiled them and mashed them up with the shells still on. It is amazing how almost any bird or animal appreciates a change of diet. Not to mention myself.

I used to eat them ten at a time, sometimes hard-boiled, sometimes in a very gaily coloured omelette, for tern eggs have slightly pink yolks.

They were the best omelettes I ever tasted.

6. The Killing of the Wild Pigs

EARLY IN JANUARY the first heavy rains drenched the island. Three months of back-breaking work lay behind me, but now at last I could begin to see some results, for I had settled down to a happy, easy, solitary—but never lonely—life. I kept my shack spotlessly clean; I had built a small lean-to on the beach, roofing it with plaited pandanus (which lasts much longer than a coconut roof) and here I sipped my evening cup of tea at the end of each day's toil. If I could not chalk up a success in my efforts to tame the fowls, at least I felt they were slowly becoming more friendly, lured on when I started offering them tern eggs. I had also begun to make a garden fence, and I had sown my seeds in shallow boxes. The breadfruit tree was flourishing; so were the two banana shoots in their squares of coconut logs. Even the cats seemed to be more contented than ordinary cats, and when the barometer started to tumble, warning me of bad weather on the way, and I buried my tool chest in its safety hole, I was able to reflect, almost placidly, that I had dry wood enough to keep a fire going for six months.

I had made careful preparations against bad weather. Two weeks' supply of uto was already cooked, and in its special box. I still had plenty of bully beef, coffee, tea, sugar, and a fair supply of flour—though it was going a bit wormy, and I had to sieve it through the invaluable tea-strainer. In truth, I had been awaiting the rain almost with impatience, not because we needed rain (for Suvarov is blessed with regular, short, sharp tropical storms) but for an entirely different and almost comical reason. Bad weather would give me my first holiday!

Does it sound ridiculous to want a "holiday" on a desert island? Believe me, I had been going at it so hard that I was even behind-hand with my reading, nor did I ever seem to have time to repair odds and ends around the house, or even to do a little mending—not clothes, but a tear in a sheet needed attention with needle and thread, and one of my canvas shoes wanted stitching; a cupboard door was loose, the books should have been taken down from their shelves and thoroughly wiped clear of mildew. Yet I never seemed to have the time. With the rainy weather, however, my outside activities would be brought to a standstill—for when it rains in the Pacific, it really does rain—and I must say I awaited the break with the excitement of a schoolboy approaching the end of term.

For over two weeks, heavy rain lashed the island, while high winds tore shrieking through the trees, and coconuts rattled on the tin roof of my shack. There was never any serious danger of hurricanes that winter, but even though I was snugly protected from the rain, nothing—not even the shield of the low jungle—could keep out what Frisbie described as "the ungodly roar" of the wind, or the twang as it sang through the taut wire guy-ropes which shuddered each time the shack trembled.

At times the wind was so fierce that when I ventured outside the torrents seemed to be driven almost horizontally. At night, particularly, I could actually see the rain through the frenzied tops of the smaller coconut trees, glittering against a thin moon, and it was hard to believe that all this water whipping past came from the heavens, for it was almost parallel to the ground, as though it spurted from some distant hosepipe with a gigantic spray.

Even though the shack didn't leak, everything seemed to be damp. Clothes, sheets, even blankets had that faint, uncomfortable feeling. The walls were wet inside as well as out, and day after day I had to wipe them down.

Outside, pools of water, with the rain dancing in them, covered the yard. The hibiscus trees by the shed had been stripped of all their blossoms, which lay at the foot of the trunks like a soggy, multi-coloured remnant of silk; the low, scudding clouds raced across the tops of the palm trees whose long fronds, writhing in the wind, looked alive and trying to escape. Even the fat, juicy paw-paw leaves, glistening with rain—my dinner plates!—were strewn over the yard like broken crockery. From time to time the clouds would lift for an hour and then a miserable but persistent sun would turn the yard into a sauna bath as the steam rose from the ground. Then the curtain of rain would come down again.

I did not go out much, except to run across the yard for some dry wood, or to get paw-paw and an occasional breadfruit, for I have never been one for indulging in unnecessary discomfort. If I did have to go out, then I made no bones about it, and did what was necessary— even though it meant getting soaked. But there was no point in going for a "pleasure" stroll when I had a comfortable shack, an extra blanket (for when it started to get cooler), a covered cook-house, plenty of food and an assortment of books. I was much better off than the city dweller who has to make his way through rain and sit in his office all day in wet trousers.

Fishing was out of the question most days, which I found almost a relief, and in fact I hardly ever went to the beach—partly because there was no point in doing so partly because the sea was the real danger, for as the winds whipped the waves into giant combers, the water came surging through the pass and over the reef with the speed of a mill race and was quite capable of rushing across Anchorage, which stood right in its path.

So, as I could not influence the angry moods of nature, I stayed indoors. I read a great deal during those days—and nights. Conrad's *Lord Jim* kept me occupied at first, especially when the screaming wind prevented me from sleeping. And then amongst the paperbacks I discovered an ancient copy of Oscar Wilde's *De Profundis* which absorbed me each evening until an accident stopped my nightly reading in bed.

It happened when a violent shudder rocked the shack, about three o'clock one morning. I thought the place was going to collapse on top of me and I jumped out of bed, fumbling for a match to light the lamp. In my haste I knocked over a tin of kerosene. It shouldn't have mattered, for the tin, of course, was unbreakable, but for some reason, in a moment of carelessness, I hadn't screwed the cap on properly. Before I could strike a match to see what I'd done, my precious kerosene was pouring out all over the floor. It was a disaster, for already I was using my second tin out of the four I had. From that day—until I devised an alternative way of lighting the shack—I gave up reading in bed.

On the other hand, the bad weather did me one good turn. During the second week, the rain virtually stopped for just one evening and I seized the opportunity to go fishing. I had to keep very close to the beach on the lagoon side of Anchorage, for heavy seas were still pounding and charging through the pass. But I managed to catch nearly two dozen ku in under an hour.

I fried some for supper, but there was a good deal

more fish than the cats or I needed and I knew they wouldn't keep fresh until morning unless they were cooked. Yet I just couldn't face the prospect of laboriously building a native oven. I was wet and cold, and everything was clammy to the touch.

On the other hand, it seemed a pity to throw away such good food, so when I had given the cats a large portion for their supper, I wrapped the rest in leaves and laid them on my new brick hearth. I don't really know what prompted me to do it—except that for once I had more fish than I needed, so instead of throwing them away, why not experiment?

The fire had gone out whilst I was fishing, but the bricks were still warm, though I could touch them without being burned, and although I was doubtful whether there was still enough heat in them, I thought the idea worth a try. It was about seven in the evening. I wrapped the fish in leaves, as usual, covered them with the "lid" of breadfruit leaves, put the two sacks on top (folded double) and weighted down with stones, and left them.

Next morning I opened up the leaf wrapping. To my surprise I found the fish were perfectly cooked and tasted far better than anything that had ever come out of my native oven. It was the continuous *low* heat which must have kept them moist and juicy. Indeed, they were so tasty that I made a hearty breakfast, watched by two reproachful cats.

After that memorable meal, I always used my brick fireplace for cooking fish in native style. Nor did I ever allow the fire to go right out.

I often lit a cigarette from the fire and in the evening livened it up for my meal, leaving it so that the bricks would keep hot whilst I was out fishing, and when I returned all I had to do was gather up the ashes and embers with a piece of tin, place the fish wrapped in leaves on the bricks, cover them and leave them for the night—and my breakfast cooked itself.

On the sixteenth day the sun was shining when I woke: the whole island steamed as it dried and when I went down to the beach the combers were already beginning to flatten out. The "holidays" were over, and it was time to get back to work.

During the rainy weather I had had plenty of time to think about the problems which still lay before me, and I decided that above all I must do something about the wild pigs, especially as during all these months the garden had never been far out of my mind. For a start I worked on a fence, an affair of stout but splintered pieces of wood which now enclosed the site awaiting its topsoil. Before I went any further, however—before I even transplanted a single seed—I knew that I must deal with the pigs.

There were five of them—five monsters dedicated to a continuous and determined onslaught on any attempt I might make at a garden. Every green thing I wanted to plant would be doomed to be gobbled up, and since a garden was a necessity, it had come to a state where it was either me or the pigs.

Occasionally I had caught a glimpse of them, but as I had no gun, there was little I could do about it. Every time I had tried to catch one, the brute would show such a turn of speed despite its cumbersome proportions that I had been left standing. For a while I toyed with the idea of constructing some sort of trap with a rope and a slip-knot, with which I could lasso them; I spent hours thinking about a deep pit covered with dry coconut fronds and leaves. But always I came back to the realisation that even were I able to snare one, the strength in those shoulders would break any rope I possessed.

It became a simple problem of survival. After a great deal of thought, I decided the only thing to do was to kill them one by one.

But even after I had made this decision, I was troubled by the best way of going about it. In the end, I decided my best hope was to spear them and the more I thought about it, the less I came to relish this gory job. Certainly I have never had any qualms about killing meat when I am hungry (and this was a great deal more serious because my whole survival seemed at stake), but whatever the reasons, the prospect of eliminating those pigs filled me with gloomy foreboding and struck me as having all the elements of being a thoroughly messy business.

Since, however, there was simply no other alternative, I started making my preparations, and during the rains I had painstakingly filed a broken machete blade until it was as sharp as a razor. This is no idle figure of speech— I could have shaved with it, and no headhunter ever possessed a more lethal spearhead. After examining it carefully, I lashed it to a stout pole.

So now I found myself equipped with a spear boasting some eleven inches of naked steel. I had the weapon, I certainly possessed the necessary determination, but now that the fine weather had returned, the problem seemed to be to lure the pigs into range one by one. From experience, I knew that a hog is seldom in the habit of looking up. So, fortified by this knowledge, I spent three days in building a platform about twelve feet up in a palm. The next couple of days I was busy hacking a clearing around the foot of the tree.

It was very simple. All I had to do now was lure the pigs. Knowing my quarry's passion for food, I waited for a bright moonlit night before opening a dozen coco-

nuts and spreading them around the base of the tree. I
then climbed into the tree and settled myself on the platform where I waited, patient but a trifle apprehensive.
My machete was close beside me. The spear shaft I
gripped in a sweaty palm.

But nothing happened; not a grunt disturbed the
silence. Night after night I seemed doomed to a vigil
amidst a tracery of fronds black against the moon. It
was romantic enough, despite my grisly preoccupation.
For four nights, as no pigs arrived, I had only to turn my
head to see the lagoon, the breakers on the reef, and
beyond that, the immensity of the ocean, with the moon
dancing on the water as though millions of needles were
cascading on its surface. It was warm and comfortable
in my tree, with the south-east trade wind purring gently,
and the only noise the jumping of mullet or the ripple
of a trevally chasing small fish in the lagoon.

Below me the moon etched eerie patterns on the ground
where the coconut crabs, some weighing up to eight
pounds, executed a grotesque dance, their huge claws
weaving and ghoulishly ripping at the white meat of the
opened nuts. A little atoll rat—one of the few spared
(so far) by Mrs. Thievery—came scampering out of the
trees, sniffed suspiciously for a moment and began
nibbling at a nut with his two long front teeth.

And then, on the fifth night, a dark shadow loomed
silently out of the tangle of creepers and vines at the edge
of the clearing, so that the little rat scuttled hurriedly
away into the outer darkness.

All at once I was aware of moonlight glinting along
tusks, accentuating the black bulk of massive shoulders.
Suddenly I was hardly able to breathe. I felt cold but
full of hatred and gripped my home-made spear more
tightly.

Approaching the first nut, the pig sniffed quietly, wary

and suspicious, because of the knowledge that an enemy was now on the island. There was a sound of chewing, another grunt, and then the boar moved on to the next nut, coming slowly closer and closer to the foot of my tree.

Normally I am a peaceable man, yet now I felt a savage sense of anticipation, and as he moved on towards the foot of my tree, I was actually trembling. My hands were aching on the shaft, the muscles of my arms were so tense they seemed to be part of the spear.

Directly below my tree, the pig paused with a deep, suspicious sniff. Instinctively I knew he had sensed me. Aiming just behind his neck, I plunged the spear downwards with all my strength. The razor-sharp metal sank in up to the shaft, and the pig gave a horrible squeal.

There came another half-human scream and the spear was wrenched from my hands. Spurting blood in the moonlight, the pig swung round with the heavy shaft sticking out of his back. As he staggered off heavily towards the thicket, I scrambled down from my platform and chased him, machete in hand.

I caught him before he reached cover and slashed my machete down across his spine. Again there came a horrible scream and as he rolled on his side, I cut his throat with one savage stroke, so that the blood flowed out to stain the coral.

Staggering back, spattered with blood, I thought for a moment I was going to be sick, but once the gurgling and thrashing stopped, once the heavy body slumped into dark shadowed immobility and I could see it lying there, I was suddenly overwhelmed with a sense of melancholy. I suppose it was the reaction. All at once, I was no longer a hunter, I was just an old man of fifty-one, alone on an atoll. I walked home slowly, deciding that I would bury the animal the following day. Nothing on earth could have induced me to eat any part of it.

As the months began to stretch out into 1953 and my garden was still in its infant stage, I was always haunted by a reluctance to dip too heavily into the meagre stores I had brought. I was desperately concerned to make them last and would only occasionally allow myself a treat like a tin of bully beef. Between these treats I simply lived off the island except, of course, for my cups of coffee and tea and the occasional pinch of curry powder or a dip into the beef dripping.

Suvarov, however, was an island capable of constant surprises. One day I came across a patch of arrowroot growing wild. It was the sort the islanders prize, since it makes better starch than any of the packets you can buy in stores. When I dug it out, I found it had a bulbous root which went nine inches down into the sand. Out of this root sprouted pale green hollow stems, with leaves rather similar to those of a paw-paw. The leaf withers when the plant matures, and this is the right moment to dig out the bulb. The ones I found on Suvarov varied enormously in size. Some were the size of small apples, whilst others weighed up to three pounds. I used this arrowroot to make poi, a very popular native dish in the South Seas. At first I mixed it with paw-paw, though later, when the garden was producing, I was to vary this with bananas or pumpkins.

It was quite a business, preparing this dish. After washing the bulbs I grated them, and then came the big operation. Earlier, I had put four pegs in the ground, not too far apart, and each about two feet high. Over these I had stretched a bit of sheeting and placed my wash basin beneath it.

On top of this sheet I piled the grated arrowroot and then poured cold water over it, stirring it with my hand until the water strained through. At first the water which drained into the bowl was milky, but with each subsequent can of water it became increasingly clear so I knew that all the starch must have been washed into the bowl leaving only a remainder of fibre on the sheet, which I threw away. When I picked up the bowl, the starch had sunk to the bottom. I poured the water off, then put the intensely white, very fine, starch into the sun to dry.

Once dried, it was easy to pound up and when I had done this, I picked a couple of nearly ripe paw-paw and diced, boiled and mashed them before mixing them with the arrowroot. I wrapped the resultant delicacy in banana leaves (making sure these wouldn't crack by drawing them over the fire to toughen them) and after that my native oven did the rest—producing a delicious pudding which I ate with coconut cream.

I depended a great deal on paw-paw before the vegetables in my garden were ready. Often when I was peckish I would cut one in half, take out the seeds but leave the skin on, then place it on my brick fireplace. Once cooked, I ate it with coconut cream, spooning it out of the shell. I remember writing in my journal that it tasted just like stewed peaches. Coconut cream which accompanied most dishes like these was easy to make. I simply split a mature nut, grated the meat as finely as possible and then wrapped it in a strip of cloth, twisting the ends until the "cream" was squeezed through.

Before long, my cook-house began to resemble a galley. In one corner stood my native oven (rarely used now), in another the uto cooker, alongside my brick fireplace with its iron bars. But all had a most necessary part in my life because the food I ate on Suvarov had to be cooked in so many different ways. Breadfruit, for instance, was always roasted on an open fire. Now the breadfruit I found on Suvarov were seldom larger than a child's football and once I had picked one from the tree all I had to do was place it on an open fire, ringed with a circle of stones to keep the wood in position. After half an hour, I turned it over so the other end could cook. It is rather hard to describe the flavour, but I am very fond of it, and had eaten it regularly when I lived in Tahiti and Moorea, where it is a staple of the Tahitians. I preferred it hot, with my own speciality, cooked coconut cream.

This was a variant of my ordinary coconut cream and I made it quite simply by filling a half coconut with cream and then dropping in a small red-hot volcanic stone which I had heated on the fire. (The bent mid-rib of a coconut frond made a serviceable pair of tongs.) The hot stone made the cream hiss and bubble, thickened it and gave it a particular piquant flavour which always seemed to go especially well with breadfruit.

Although I fished every day, there were only two occasions when I encountered sharks. The first time was near the north end of the island, where I had noticed a big pool fed with a continual flood of sea which seemed to well up from a gap in the reef.

It looked a likely place for fish and I took a couple of steps into the pool, rod in hand.

Without a moment's warning, three sharks were charging towards me. Each looked about three feet long —the type which thrives in comparatively shallow water. For a moment I was almost paralysed and then instinctively I backed hastily out of the pool, banging the water furiously with my rod. It was only a matter of two or three steps, but those seconds seemed a long, long time. Fortunately, my desperately thrashing rod seemed to scare the sharks, who turned away. After that, I took care to cross the pool where the water was only ankle-deep.

The second occasion was a great deal more dangerous. One moonlit night I was standing in two feet of water fishing for ku with my bamboo rod when a big fish took the lure in a whirl of spray.

I had no idea what he was, but slowly and carefully I worked him to the edge of the reef, and when I realised he was well hooked, I leaned forward cautiously to grip him by the gills.

My hand was within six inches of his head when some instinct made me hesitate. Even now I do not know what it was, other than some subconscious mechanism which must have warned me of imminent danger.

That second saved my life. While the big fish was still struggling on my line, a great grey mass rushed on me like a torpedo. There was no time to move, no time even to panic. Before I could draw my hand away, a smashing blow whacked me across both legs, throwing me over on to my back.

I jumped up, gasping for breath and spitting out salt water. The fish was gone. The lure had vanished. I could see my bamboo rod floating in the water. The shark must have missed my hand by inches as it took the fish, and in passing had hit me with its tail.

I walked slowly back to the shack. The skin on my left leg was as rough as if I had rubbed sandpaper across it.

By the late spring of 1953 I had killed the last of the pigs. It had taken all that time because I'd had to wait for moonlit nights. I was forced to repeat the horrible business four more times—perched in my lonely tree with the moon rippling peaceably over the lagoon, and my lethal spear in my hand. Each time the same macabre scene was re-enacted, sometimes swiftly, sometimes after an infinity of waiting.

I hated those gory nights so much that I had to force myself to climb the tree, and I would breathe a sigh of relief when occasionally dark clouds obliterated the moon and made it impossible for me to keep my vigil.

But at the end of it, in the weeks following the finale of the whole brutal business, the change was astonishing. Wild paw-paw shoots sprang up everywhere, seeded from the trees the pigs had been unable to kill. The wild bananas began to flourish. And it was then—fortified with the knowledge that any garden I made now would be safe—that I finally decided I must try and mend the leaky old tub of a boat the coast-watchers had left, and which still lay on my veranda. I might well have left her undisturbed for years had I not urgently needed topsoil for my garden. Since this lay in plenty at the south end of the island, there was just no choice. I could not face the prospect of carrying sack after sack on my back a quarter of a mile to the garden.

"Neale," I told myself firmly one day, "what you need now is a boat."

Would the old tub stand the strain? I decided it was worth a try. Quite aside from the fact that if I got her afloat I would be able to ferry loads of soil for the garden, I knew that once she was seaworthy I could sail to Motu Tuo, six miles across the lagoon, or any other of the small islets in the fifty square miles of water inside the reef.

I looked her over carefully. Frankly, she was not impressive—ten feet long and three feet wide, a most ungainly, flat-bottomed craft. Her sides were in fairly good shape, but her keel of three-inch thick twelve-inch long planks showed gaping quarter-inch cracks between each pair of planks.

However was I going to caulk her? What a fool I had been not to bring some oakum! I suddenly remembered a length of two-inch thick rope which I had found after the *Mahurangi* sailed and had stored away in the shed. Getting it out, I found it to be about fifteen feet long, and I cut it into yard-long pieces which I teased strand by strand until I had something which resembled a supply of oakum. I made a rough paint brush with another bit of old rope and got to work on the ruin. Working on the veranda, I doused the open seams with plenty of green paint and then caulked them with my home-made oakum, taking care not to drive it in too hard, since that would have been fatal at this stage.

Once my handiwork was dry, I turned the boat upside down and filled the seams on the outer side with more thick layers of green paint. Then I nailed on two ten-foot lengths of wood I had cut, again well painted, so they entirely covered the seams. The next thing was to turn the boat the right way again, and now I used one of my flat pieces of iron as a caulking tool and hammered the caulking down as tightly as I could, topping it up with more alternate layers of paint and oakum until the seams were entirely filled. Finally I painted the seams over again and puttied them whilst the paint was still wet.

I must have done a really good job, for once I launched her she never leaked, and once I was satisfied she was seaworthy, I named her in red paint on her stern the *Ruptured Duckling* in memory of an old friend in Tahiti whose canoe had borne the same name.

The *Ruptured Duckling*, ungainly and difficult though she was, proved invaluable; and soon I was towing her through the shallows to the south end of the island where

I would spend a day gathering soil. I could haul a full load back in an hour or two—a load which would have taken me days to carry on my back.

But the *Ruptured Duckling* also opened up a new world to me. For now if I felt like a change I could row over to one of the islets where I indulged in my favourite hobby of looking for flotsam. I found all kinds of things; odd Japanese rubber shoes—the sort with a piece of rubber or plastic to stick between the toes—bottles, tins, bits of iron ballast.

One day I came on something which indicated a vessel must recently have been very close to the island. The sight of a green coconut lying among the stones on Brushwood Islet gave me an odd feeling. Picking it up, I discovered one end had been cut off—the wrong end, where the eyes had been.

"That must have been the work of some popaa," I said to myself, using the native dialect for European. No native would open a drinking nut like this at the eye-end where the husk is thickest. I could see the work had been done clumsily too, with a blunt knife.

When I opened the nut there was still some soft clean white meat. It could not have been in the sea for more than a couple of days and must have been thrown overboard from a vessel passing very close to the island.

"Why didn't they call in?" I wondered. It would have been pleasant to see a friendly face and I remember thinking that I might have been able to swap some island produce for a tin of kerosene—and start reading in bed again, for that was a pleasure I really missed.

I cannot remember how my thoughts remained on the subject of reading in bed after I'd seen that coconut, nor can I say why one day some weeks later it suddenly occurred to me that I might be able to make some candles out of the chunks of wax I had found months previously. Perhaps, after all, it had nothing to do with finding that coconut, but when one day I broke a few bits off one piece of wax and discovered they would melt at a low heat, it seemed quite feasible to make candles. Nothing could be more welcome since I was always frightened of running out of kerosene and used it so sparingly that I usually moved around at night without any light at all.

Candle-making did not prove all that difficult, but I needed bamboo, which did not grow on Suvarov. From time to time, however, I picked up broken pieces on the beach which must have been washed ashore, presumably thrown overboard from Japanese fishing boats.

Selecting one, I cut it into sections into which I could easily pour the melted wax. What troubled me now was what to use for a wick. I solved this problem by boring tiny holes, spaced six inches apart, into a piece of old planking, then I threaded a piece of string through each hole, knotting each one so it could not be pulled right through.

I stood a section of hollow bamboo over each hole. The string I now drew through each piece of bamboo was meant to be the wick but I had a real job keeping this sufficiently taut, especially as I had both hands occupied holding the bamboo and pouring in the melted wax. After several abortive attempts to keep the "wick" in the centre of the hollow bamboo, I tied the top of each piece of string to the middle of a nail. When I laid it across the top of the empty bamboo the string was centred and then, by turning the nail, I was able to tighten the string and keep it in the centre, while I poured in the melted wax—not quite to the top, so that some wick still showed.

It took nearly half an hour for the wax to set; once I was sure it was hard, I cut the knots under the wooden board, carefully split the bamboo in half—and there were my candles.

After this, I never had occasion to use the table lamp again. I was able to keep my precious kerosene for the hurricane lamp which sooner or later I knew was going to be vital when the time came again to go outside in bad weather.

Those candles lasted for years. And the very next evening I started reading in bed again.

7. Gardening—and a Chicken "Farm"

ONCE THE pigs were out of the way I was able to start on my garden in earnest, for I had decided I must get it ready and plant out my seeds before I even thought of building a fowl run. The fence was finished and I had already started bringing up a little topsoil from the south end of the island. I knew exactly where the best soil was. Each morning I rowed to the south end of the island, beached the *Ruptured Duckling* and started inland, carrying my shovel and some sugar bags.

Getting this soil for the garden was one of the most laborious tasks I ever had to tackle. Quite apart from the back-breaking work of digging it up, sacking it and rowing or pulling it back in the boat, I discovered that the stuff was very patchy and contained so many coral pebbles that I was forced to sieve it.

Obviously this had to be done on the spot where I dug out the topsoil, so I constructed a sieve by tacking a double layer of half-inch netting to a rectangular wooden frame about two feet long and eighteen inches wide, with sides about six inches high. This looked solid enough, but the weight of stones quickly threatened to knock the bottom out, so I fastened two pieces of baling wire, drawn taut, from corner to corner diagonally, and crossing in the centre. After that my sieve never let me down.

I scraped rather than dug the soil—if you could call it

soil—into small heaps, which I sieved a couple of shovelfuls at a time and packed into sugar bags. I counted it a good day's work if I were able to fill four or five bags, which I then carried down to the boat. Over the next few weeks I collected more than a hundred bags of topsoil from this part of the island, each one of which I had to lug to the boat. Next I had to row or pull the heavily-laden *Duckling* back through the shallow water, unload the bags and carry them one by one to the garden.

It was on one of these topsoil expeditions that I noticed a wild duck, perched on a mushroom of coral and looking very bedraggled, as indeed she had the right to be after what must have been a journey of at least two hundred miles.

I was astounded, for apart from frigates, terns and a few bosun birds—lords of the Pacific with their scarlet tails and white plumage—no living thing had ever alighted before on Suvarov whilst I had been there, and I can remember the tingle of excitement as I set down my shovel and sacks and started to walk towards her. In a way I was surprised (knowing myself only too well by now) that I was not in any way impelled by a hunter's instinct. It never entered my head to ponder how good (if slightly fishy) she would taste after a few hours in the stewpot.

Looking on that first moment—from which a long and curious friendship, complicated by a strange mixture of trust and temptation, was to develop—I cannot imagine why I felt such a tender interest in that bird. I like animals and birds well enough and hate the casual cruelty which seems so prevalent towards them in the islands. But just the same I was hardly the sort of man to start investing them with the human attributes which seem to have become so fashionable since Walt Disney started putting words into their mouths.

As far as I am concerned (up to that moment, I mean) animals or birds had always been things to be kept in their proper place. In other words, if I were hungry, the unfortunate creature destined for my pot would be killed with as little compunction as a Chicago meat packer might kill a heifer and yet be a sidesman in church each Sunday.

But the wild duck was to prove quite different. As I stepped to within some fifteen paces, she became frightened and flew off twenty yards or so, then perched lonely and forlorn, observing me suspiciously. When I slowly approached her again she waited until I was exactly the same distance away, then slowly flew off another twenty yards or so.

I returned to my shovel and sacks, and continued scraping the thin layer of topsoil into small heaps.

And then, for the time being, I forgot her, and rowed back to the garden which was sited just behind the house. The coast-watchers must have chosen this spot for two reasons. Firstly, it was sheltered from any wind; and secondly, the paw-paw tree had been growing there for some time. It was a pleasant place, the square of earth now fenced in and shaded by a few tall coconuts and the spiky leaves of pandanus trees. Once I had got things really under way, I planned to have my fruit and vegetables growing close together.

The seeds which I had set out in boxes were now growing so quickly that they were almost ready for planting and I had quite a race to bring in the last of the topsoil. Now that the pigs were gone everything thrived outrageously. Even before I had finished the garden fence I had planted paw-paw shoots around the inside at ten-foot intervals, and these too were shooting up at such amazing speed that I wondered whether the gardener would ever be able to keep pace with his plants.

My journal of those days is filled with passages which even now I fancy hardly give an idea of the enormous amount of work I had to put in. There were so many incidental jobs there never seemed time to relax. And in the months which followed, time seemed to slip away; for my day-to-day life had long since settled into a sort of rhythm and pattern, starting with my early morning breakfast and ending with tea on the beach and a read in bed.

All sorts of unexpected incidents kept cropping up. Do you remember the splutter of amazement my friend in Raro had given when I insisted on taking my bicycle pump to Suvarov? Well, it came in very useful, for as I noted in my journal, "Nobody would think there would be a use for a bicycle pump on the island, but I used one with, I hope, good advantage today. A young breadfruit tree, about ten feet high near the garden is badly infested with White Aphis or Mealy Bug, and the black rust mites (a sooty-like deposit): true name unknown to me. I sprayed it with about three gallons of soapy water which I used this morning to boil bed-clothes. The bicycle pump made an excellent spray."

Or there was the inevitable moment on the home front when I noted "There was a case of incest today as Mrs. Thievery and Mr. Tom-Tom are, in fact, mother and son. I shall have some drowning to do as two cats are enough to keep down the few rats."

There were uneasy moments too. Unexpectedly, I went down with a minor bout of fever—" Last night after turning in, I felt chilly and a pain started in my right groin, so I dosed myself with Sulph. Thiazole and sure enough it turned out to be a fever. Have been in bed all day. I'm sure the fever was caused by a fish-bone I stepped on a couple of days ago. Still feel pretty shaky and have eaten nothing today."

These bouts were to return but, fortunately, this one cleared up quickly and within two days I was back at work again. I must have made a fairly rapid recovery, for the day after I left my bed I made my biggest catch on the reef so far—four crayfish and a cod.

Two of the crays were big and one had such enormous legs that I had difficulty in pulling him out. I noted, "A sea broke over me and if I hadn't been anchored to the cray with both hands, I'd have been washed away. As it was, I nearly lost the spear. The big fellow was in a smooth, round cavity under a ledge, otherwise I'd never have got him out."

I had not seen the wild duck for some days now although the place where I first encountered her was where I always went to collect the best topsoil, and I was often down at the southern tip of the island gathering soil. One day, although I can't remember how it came about, I had put some scraps of uto in an old cigarette tin after feeding the fowls, and now, after beaching the *Duckling* I noticed the tin in the bottom of the boat. Subconsciously I must have brought it for the wild duck.

And there she was; almost as though she were waiting for me, or so I flattered myself, and I realised then just how anxious I had been to see whether or not she had flown away from the island.

At the time I never thought that my behaviour was in any way odd. Looking back on it, I imagine it must have sprung from a loneliness of which I had never been aware until this minute.

It was hopeless trying to get up close to her. I spread out the uto, and walked up to the patch of topsoil and began sieving and shovelling it into the sugar bags. Out of the corner of my eye, however, I watched her every movement.

I had half an hour to wait. All this time she remained there motionless. Then she slowly waddled over to the uto and began to gobble it up. It must have been at that moment I made up my mind that providing she did not fly away, I would not rest content until I had succeeded in taming her.

I had other pressing tasks to attend to and did not return to the south end of the island for some days. Indeed, there was so much on my mind that I had temporarily forgotten her and was astonished when she appeared in the yard one evening. I noticed her over in the far corner where there were some clumps of grass with seed heads, and she was running her bill over them to extract the seeds. I stood there for a moment, watching; then I walked towards her. She watched me until I was about twenty paces from her before she half-turned and waddled obliquely away, still eyeing me all the time.

For some time now I had been splitting half a dozen sprouting nuts every evening to encourage the fowls to feel at home near the shack. I had not yet started to build their run so they came and went just as they pleased. There were several of them about now and the next evening the wild duck joined them. She still refused to let me near her so I walked away. Every evening the same thing happened. She would come into the yard, watch me suspiciously—and then, after a week or so, she was starting to waddle among the split uto and nibbling at them. She seemed to be a little wary of the fowls squabbling among themselves as usual. I started spacing the split nuts farther apart, then stood at a good distance, watching.

So it went on. I was unable to get anywhere near

taming her for quite a while, despite the fact she now seemed to be making herself quite at home. Then one evening I decided to grate some coconut, put it in an old butter tin, and place a tin of water beside it. I had noticed that though she obviously liked uto it was always difficult for her to extract it from the nut because, unlike a hen, she couldn't peck at it.

She made straight for the two tins—almost as though she had been expecting them—and with an almost comical meticulousness she drank from the water after each mouthful of grated coconut. Now each evening I positioned myself a little closer to the tins.

If progress at taming the duck was slow but sure, everything else seemed to move with remarkable speed, and by the end of spring the garden was at last ready. It had taken months to bring up all the topsoil but now the final load had been spread out and I had manured it with humus from the three tree boxes, working it into the soil with a rake made out of palm fronds—or rather a series of rakes, for they did not last very long.

In the new layer of soil I planted out some sixty tomatoes, three rows of shallots, some rock melons, water melons, pumpkins, cucumbers, Indian vine, three rows of kumeras (or yams). Now all I had to do was await my first crops. Or so I thought.

For some weeks I had been getting increasingly annoyed by the stupidity of the fowls, and now that I had planted out my garden, I decided to set about taming them and providing myself with a regular supply of eggs and roosters for the Sunday stewpot.

Searching for eggs, taming the fowls, and constructing a run were three vital but time-consuming activities which went hand in hand, but with such eventual success that by the time I left Suvarov the fowl population had increased to forty strong, despite inroads for my larder. Indeed, my "flock" became a blessing and a standby later on whenever it was difficult to obtain uto or pawpaw—or, on stormy days, fish—for then the fowls and their eggs were all I had (apart from coconuts) to keep me alive.

But that was all in the future. Meantime, I was still having a major headache finding any eggs, for the birds had been running wild for years now and nothing seemed to delight them more than cackling loudly once they had removed themselves as far as possible from the spot where they had actually laid. Like a schoolboy going bird's-nesting, I would spend hours during those first months stealthily tracking my hens in a determined effort to discover their nests.

Living on a motu as small as Anchorage, one would have thought that no nest could remain hidden for long; one might have thought, too, that a bird the size of a hen might have experienced some difficulty in making itself invisible. But this did not prove to be the case and my fowls seemed to look on egg-laying as so intensely private that they went to extraordinary lengths to keep their affairs secret. The roosters, too, on whom I had designs for my cooking pot became remarkably elusive. Three entries from my 1953 journal show I was succumbing to a disease which was obviously endemic on Suvarov. I called it "egg frustration."

". . . Wasted time following the hen that lays away. She went in a wide semi-circle and finally eluded me. I waited for half an hour to see if she would return. Not a sign; nor did she cackle again. She was in the yard when I returned. Am determined to find her nest, besides now I've got to show something for the time wasted looking . . . ."

". . . Tried to follow the same hen but a young rooster upset her. I chased him and only managed to scare the hen. She wouldn't go straight to the nest but hung around in the bush. Couldn't waste any more time so vowed I would put that young rooster in the pot. Don't like his crow anyhow. Caught him when his back was to me. He was too busy to notice me . . . ."

". . . At last discovered her nest with ten eggs. This morning she had started making a noise so I followed her. Suddenly she disappeared. I couldn't believe my eyes, so waited a bit longer and investigated a coconut stump about ten feet high. Damn me, if I didn't see her head sticking out of a hole four feet from the ground. Talk about pigs not thinking to look up—I'm as bad! A lot of writing about nothing, but I feel I've achieved a major victory . . . ."

Of course, it was not a "major victory" at all and the unending waste of time soon convinced me that the only way to triumph over these elusive fowls was to build a good strong run and pen them in; as a matter of fact I had already made a tentative start whilst preparing the garden.

There was no point in completing the fowl run until I had succeeded in luring the birds to the spot I had selected in order to make them feel at home. Otherwise, even with a brand-new run, my whole plan would collapse since I'd never manage to round them up and drive them in. Week after week I set about this lengthy task. I laid out all the split uto in the new spot. The birds were bright enough to come and get it and seemed to thrive on these young sprouting coconuts. But at first the exasperatingly stupid creatures did not seem to grasp the idea that their meals were being served up at regular times. One or two near at hand would come clucking and running when I turned up, but the others would stay pecking about in the undergrowth, scratching for food, quite oblivious to the fact that a feast was served, and ready to eat, almost under their beaks. I tried coaxing them with a fine range of farmyard sounds, but the stupid birds did not seem to understand English. I tried to get behind them and shoo them towards the food, but as soon as I did this, off they ran, squawking protests, in the opposite direction. There is nothing so frustrating as an old hen.

Eventually, I hit on a solution so ridiculously simple— and so much more appropriate for humans than hens— that it still makes me laugh when I think of it. I banged a gong for breakfast and tea! It was as simple as that.

Morning and evening from that moment on I scattered the split uto nuts on the square of ground where the run was to be built, and then banged lustily on the old iron crowbar made from the transmission shaft of a Model T Ford I had acquired in a Raro junkyard. The result was really extraordinary. Up till now I had spent weeks unsuccessfully trying to cajole the fowls into a regular feeding time. Now, within a week, they were recognising the familiar sound of the beaten crowbar, and came running as fast as they could, determined not to miss a good feed. They brought all sorts of surprises with them, too—in the shape of at least two clutches of chicks which I had no idea even existed. Although this achievement did not immediately solve my egg-collecting problems, at least I was able to keep track of the island's hen population, and now I started building the chicken run in earnest.

Firstly I made a rough shelter and thatched it over with coconut fronds. Then I fixed up some perches inside, and used some pieces of flattened-out old corrugated iron to fashion a tray underneath them which would collect the droppings to make splendid manure for my garden.

Next, I built a fence. This was a laborious job, for I

had to gather hundreds of fallen coconut fronds and strip off their leaves with my machete before I could cut their mid-ribs into six-foot lengths. These mid-ribs are widest at the base so, using bits of old baling wire, I fastened them together alternately—one base at the bottom, one at the top—to make them fit more closely. The next step was a gate made from odd bits of wire netting lashed on to a wooden frame, and hinged with more wire anchored to a solid post.

Building the fowl run took me several weeks, and all this time I was occupied with other jobs which were vital to keep me going. Sometimes bad weather would hold me up for days, but however difficult things seemed, I never lost sight of my purpose.

There was another reason too. The hens had grown to hate the wild duck. On several occasions I had noticed them waiting for her to come into the yard and, as though according to some pre-arranged plan, they would attack her.

I never really discovered the reason for this jealousy— perhaps it lay in some strange animal awareness that she was always free to fly away. If hens are capable of thought (which I doubt), I suspect the real reason was her intrusion into the yard they now regarded as their private domain.

During these last weeks I had come a long way towards taming the duck. By now she would allow me within five paces of her—maybe because she had become so dependent on her evening meal.

"The wild duck is making herself at home all right," I wrote. "I still put grated coconut in a tin and a tin of water alongside. She takes a mouthful of nut, then dips her bill in the water—does it with every mouthful. Her wing feathers look a bit the worse for wear, so I expect she's not young. She spends the greater part of her day in the shade, standing on one leg, with her head thrown back, sleeping, but with one eye open; then disappears just before sunset. Mr. Tom-Tom has stalked her a couple of times. I've had to speak to him sharply about that."

I often wondered where she spent the night. Until now I had never seen her fly away, but one evening I had just left the bath-house when I noticed her waddling towards the lagoon. Instinctively I sensed she had some definite purpose. I stood and watched.

As soon as she had reached the edge of the clearing where the ground sloped down to the lagoon, she took off, flying low—a few feet only above the ground— between the coconut trees towards the beach. From then on she changed course, heading out over the lagoon and making for Whale Islet, three-quarters of a mile away. A few evenings later I saw her do the same thing again—and she never varied this habit, but flew precisely the same course through the trees and over the water.

I must not give the impression that I thought about the duck all the time, but I did wonder occasionally how I could tame her. It's hard to explain why I should have thought about it at all, for I can imagine no duller pet than a duck—and, after all, I did have my cats. I suppose it was another challenge—something as simple as that. I was already beginning to get eggs, the garden was growing, and possibly (though I didn't realise it at the time) I did not now have to work quite so hard. Whatever the reason, I did—from time to time—toy with the idea of making a more positive attempt to tame her.

And in the end it came about quite by chance, without any thought, without any planning. One day she was distant and suspicious, the next she was eating out of my hand. And to this day I cannot explain why or how it happened. I can only assume that it was a question of time which had built up her confidence in me.

Almost without thinking, I held out my hand one evening with a little grated nut in my palm. She came up to me without the slightest hesitation and immediately started feeding. To my amazement, she now seemed completely unafraid and after that I fed her every day, with the result that she became so used to this routine that she would become quite angry if I were a few minutes late!

"I really had to laugh today," I wrote, "for I was a bit late reaching the shack to prepare the duck's food and she came towards me with one solitary disapproving quack."

After that there was always a disapproving quack if I should be late with her supper. Never two quacks— just the one.

Soon she would follow me up to the veranda, almost like a dog. She was a creature of precise habit, and never appeared in the yard before feeding time. Never once was there a note of disapproval so long as I was on time. At other times I saw her on the beach and sometimes I caught a glimpse of her thirty or forty feet out in the lagoon when it was calm, asleep with her head tucked under her wing.

My work on the fowl run was rudely interrupted by another bout of fever, which prostrated me in a matter of hours after I had scratched my foot on some coral. Nothing could have been more frustrating. Since I had been on the island I had never even had a cold or a runny nose, despite often being soaked to the skin and chilled at nights when the weather changed unexpectedly. I felt sure my immunity was due to an absence of germs on the island. Now I come to think of it, I had read somewhere that the Americans living at the South Pole never caught what is called "the common cold" except when a parcel from a relative in the States had been parachuted down to the tiny camp, accompanied by unwelcome germs.

The fever was a very different matter. I had had touches of fever in the Islands before, so when I was struck down by this attack I was not unduly worried and simply staggered to the safety of my bed. Sure enough, it passed off after a day or so, leaving me a little weak, but with no serious after-effects.

Nonetheless, it was not exactly pleasant. And lying there I recalled the jagged coral spike which had penetrated the heel of my shoe. It was nothing more than a scratch, which didn't even need a bandage. Yet within twenty-four hours, here I was with a raging temperature. It had been almost all I could manage to crawl shakily to my bed and lie there. I would have to be careful—otherwise I might get a really bad bout.

Once the fever had burned itself out, I remember I staggered down to Pylades Bay for a swim as though to restore and cleanse myself in its warm, clear water. And on the way back, I stopped to look at my garden; for during the weeks I had spent building the fowl run, I had also tended the plants assiduously, staking out the tomatoes which were now three feet tall, and stringing up the other plants as they started to blossom. Though I had lost one or two plants from crabs which managed to claw their way through the fence, the rest had grown with astonishing speed, with foliage so thick and dense I had to trim all the lower leaves. I walked back to my shack well satisfied. Within a very short time I could expect my first fruit and vegetables, for everything seemed to be going splendidly.

And then I was threatened with near disaster. The fruit refused to set! Plants I had confidently expected to see loaded with fruit produced nothing more than a couple of small tomatoes.

I noted gloomily in my journal, "the rock melons and the kumeras I have planted are growing vigorously and are full of flowers, but the fruit won't set; it just forms, then turns yellow and drops off. The same goes for the water melons. Must be the lack of bees. Hardly any of the tomatoes have fruit. If all the flowers set they would be loaded. I picked two today that had started to ripen. I shall soon replant the kumeras. So far they have been a failure."

The only things which grew well were my shallots, but even here I seemed to be dogged with bad luck, and it was quite a while before I had the chance to taste one because they simply vanished. At first I couldn't understand it. A young shoot had only to appear above ground in the evening to be mysteriously gone next morning. Night after night I kept a close and suspicious watch on the hens. But it wasn't in character; they were too frightened, and certainly too dim-witted to have forced a way through the fence. I wondered about the coconut crabs, but there were hardly any on the island by now, and in any case they were far too big to get through the fence.

Shortly before tea one evening I was walking along the garden when I smelt a strong scent of onions. Not baby shallots, but a really strong onion smell. I went to investigate—and found my answer. Rows of my precious plants were lying uprooted on a bare patch of ground near the onion bed. And round the plants, scores and scores of hermit crabs—some as tiny as a thumb nail—were having the feast of their lives.

Here was the secret of the vanishing onions. The crabs were so tiny they could get through any fence; the bigger ones, lured on by the tantalising smell of onions already uprooted, were actually capable of climbing slowly and painfully *over* the fence.

Gardening—and a Chicken "Farm"

There was only one thing to do. Fortunately, hermit crabs tend to stay in one spot and they cannot move quickly. Next evening I laid out coconut bait near the onion bed and when I went down there towards sunset with an old tin, I pounced on and collected over a hundred victims—which I left in the tin until morning, when I took them down near the southern tip of the island and threw them into the bush. There was no point in killing them, they were too far away ever to return. Each night for over a week I repeated this performance until there were none left.

At least I had a few shallots, but the rest of the garden was such a miserable failure that I could have wept with despair. All that painstaking work had been for nothing. All that topsoil I had carried so laboriously from the south end had produced nothing more than a few pitiful blossoms which yellowed and died without producing any of the fruit and vegetables I needed so badly.

The curious thing is that—though I am *supposed* to be a handyman—it was some time before it struck me that instead of sitting back and moaning about ill-luck I might be able to pollinate the blossoms myself. Why not? I had never been a gardener for the simple reason that more than enough of everything grows wild in the South Seas; but one of the few fascinating paperback books left by the coast-watchers was an abridged edition of Darwin's *The Origin of Species*. I had read it with enormous interest, and now remembered the passages in which he had described how the bees and other insects had pollinated flowers.

There was only one thing to be done. Since there were no bees, I would pollinate the blossoms by hand—and I set about it the very next day.

It was not as difficult as you might imagine, for there were usually more male than female flowers, and I could distinguish them easily as the pollen-bearing stamens in the male blossoms were usually longer. All I had to do in most cases was break off a male flower and rub the pollen on to the female flower.

The easiest of all were the pumpkins, for the male flower had extra long stamens and the female flower a definite orifice into which I could push the pollen, up and down, to make sure of fertilisation.

The tomatoes proved the most reluctant. I took a matchstick and bound some very fine, almost hair-like feathers of a bosun bird with cotton on to the end to make a miniature brush. Since I found it virtually impossible to distinguish the female from the male blossoms as they hung in clusters on the plants, the best I could do was to brush from flower to flower without taking off any blossoms. I went over the whole tomato crop two or three times, first one way, then another, and it worked.

Once I had fertilised the blossoms, I enjoyed some excellent crops. In three months I was picking tomatoes; in four months pumpkins and wonderful melons, both canteloupe and rock melons.

And now everything seemed to settle into place, as I had always imagined it would. Soon the fowl run was "inhabited," and once the garden was yielding and the hens laying, I became almost self-sufficient. From this moment I had more fish than I needed, plenty of fruit and vegetables and a regular rooster for the pot.

Nonetheless, I never succeeded in rounding up all the fowls inside my run. In fact, I never pushed this too far because hens are stubborn and some of the more independent-minded might have become actually unhappy in their new surroundings and consequently gone "on strike." But the others seemed happy enough and inside the run a new batch of chicks was growing at full speed.

Every afternoon I let out my new flock to forage for

greenstuffs. In no time they had discovered worms and insects, and often chased—frequently catching—small island lizards. Fowls need greenstuffs to remain healthy and the yolks of my eggs were always a good colour— quite different from the anaemic yellow of the "mechanised" eggs shipped from New Zealand to Rarotonga.

But though the eggs tasted good, I must admit I hardly enjoyed the roosters. It was essential I should eat them to give me a balanced diet, but thinking back to those days, I feel I never want to eat a rooster again. What hours I spent cutting them up for the cooking pot; what countless times I ate those tasteless, insipid birds merely because I was even more bored with fish.

At first it was not too bad. I had flour and fat, so I could make a passable "Southern Fried Chicken" if I felt so inclined. But once these tasty additions were all used up there was only one way to cook it. I cut the wretched bird into pieces, put it in the pot and added two or three shallots from my garden for flavouring. Although they added *something* to the taste, it is not a recipe I recommend to the wife anxious to prove the way to her man's heart is through his stomach.

Unlike me, Mr. Tom-Tom and Mrs. Thievery loved their weekly chicken. Since their normal diet was solid fish, they soon came to recognise the smell floating out of the pot. Sundays for them were different in the only way that matters to cats, and both of them exhibited an uncanny sense of timing, even on the Saturday they sensed a rooster was due to be killed. From then on they were constantly in evidence around the cook-house, even sitting unblinkingly by the box where I kept the rooster, patient in the sure knowledge that sooner or later the time would come for Sunday lunch.

8. My First Visitors

On August 4, 1953—ten months after I had landed —I welcomed my first visitors.

It was unexpected because I had long since stopped wondering whether one day I would wake up to discover a strange yacht or schooner anchored in the lagoon. I had become so engrossed with my life on Suvarov that I rarely gave a thought to the outside world.

They were very happy days. I was never lonely, though now and again I would walk along the reef wishing somebody could be with me—not because I wanted company but just because all this beauty seemed too perfect to keep to myself.

That August day happened to be particularly beautiful. A light easterly breeze was blowing and around two in the afternoon I took my spear and sauntered out along the reef, not really to catch fish, but more for the walk. After I had strolled a little way, the day struck me as so especially calm and perfect that I stopped and turned round to look along the shoreline.

There, in the shimmering distance, was a sail. I stared in momentary disbelief, but there it was, one of the most beautiful sights the Pacific can ever offer—a ship in full sail edging her way through the blue waters. She was plainly making for the entrance to the lagoon. It was so long since I had seen a sail that it took an appreciable time for the reality to sink in, for me to realise that in an hour or two I would actually be talking to other people; men, perhaps women; talking to them, instead of to myself!

Once I was over the initial surprise and excitement, a practical but prosaic thought came into my mind. It was not "I wonder who they can be?" nor "Will they be planning to stay?" On the contrary, as I walked back to the shack, the slender link still tethering me to civilisation had grown suddenly stouter and tighter so that I thought "I wonder if they've come from Rarotonga and if they've brought any mail?"

Before I reached the shack, the vessel had lowered her sail and was entering the passage under auxiliary power. I hurried inside to change my strip of pareu for a pair of shorts in case there were ladies aboard.

By the time I had come out again she had dropped anchor in thirty feet of water about a hundred yards off the old pier, and I remember how another thought suddenly struck me—that the pier which had been smashed up in the 1942 hurricane was an eyesore, and it was high time I tidied it up.

I could see now that the vessel was a single-masted forty-foot yacht, but I resisted the temptation to wave or shout and rush down the beach to meet my visitors. I decided to give them a little while to settle down before rowing out in the *Ruptured Duckling*.

As I pushed the *Duckling* off the beach and into the water, I could see four people crowding the rails of the yacht. They waved, but of course as soon as I began rowing across the lagoon my back was turned towards them, so I did not really see them until a few moments later when I came alongside, and two men were helping me to make fast the dinghy whilst two women looked on. Then I was aboard—and within a few minutes was drinking tea brewed by somebody else for the first time in ten months. And with milk in it!

The elder of the two held out a hand. "My name's Tom Worth." He was approaching middle age, looked very fit, without a spare ounce of flesh.

"And I'm Mrs. Worth," said a slender lady who looked very pleasant.

"I'm Tom Neale," I replied, wondering whether Dr. Livingstone had felt as tongue-tied when Stanley introduced himself, for I had often pictured this precise moment—the exact moment of meeting strangers—and I had contemplated it with a certain nervousness. After all, what could one say to strangers? Especially as they would probably regard me with the suspicion normally reserved for a mental case.

There was a moment of almost embarrassed silence and then Tom Worth said something that staggered me— and broke the ice.

"Oh yes!" He laughed cheerfully. "We know all about you!" He turned to his two younger passengers, and introduced them as Mr. and Mrs. Taylor.

Whilst Mrs. Worth poured out the tea I asked how they had come to find out about me being here. "The British Consul in Tahiti told me," Tom Worth explained. "I believe he's an old friend of yours. You know what he said? Call in at Suvarov and see whether or not Tom Neale has kicked what remains of the island into the sea with those big boots of his."

Those boots! I remember the day the British Consul in Papeete asked why I wore such big boots in such a hot climate. It was in order to strengthen a weak ankle after an accident, but these boots became a stock joke between us from that moment onwards.

"Would you like some more tea, Mr. Neale?" Mrs. Worth's casual question jerked me from my memories of Tahiti into reality—if this were reality. For how incongruous it all seemed! Surreptitiously I watched this slim, good-looking woman pouring tea, while Mrs. Taylor, with a smile, proffered the milk (out of a jug!) and sugar. We might have been a thousand miles from Suvarov.

I liked Worth and his wife immediately. He was one of those easy-going individuals whom you automatically think of in Christian name terms, and before long we were Tom to each other. The younger Taylors were also delightful. I gathered that they were friends who had come along for the trip, and Taylor was soon asking me "Is the fishing good? Any chance of going out together?" I promised him we would go out with spears the following day.

After my third cup, Mrs. Worth asked, with a diffidence I found most pleasing, "We don't want to disturb you, but we'd love to see your island before it gets dark."

It was the way she slightly accented *your* island that made me jump up full of apologies for my lack of hospitality. Soon we were all rowing ashore.

They seemed fascinated, and it was a pleasant feeling as I showed them round the shack and the yard, to realise that they seemed to be enjoying my company as much as I was enjoying theirs. Mrs. Worth particularly was intrigued. She examined the cook-house with all its various contraptions, and when I wrapped some ku in banana leaves, and put them in the hearth to cook in time for tomorrow's breakfast, she called her husband.

"Why can't *you* do that at home?" she laughed.

The ladies insisted on examining every corner of the shack. Mrs. Taylor seemed to be a great reader and was soon thumbing through my books.

"Did you choose all these?" She pointed to the motley selection of paperbacks on my office shelf and when I shook my head, she added, "I thought not. They don't *look* you—not all of them, anyway."

So I had to explain how the coast-watchers had left them, and then while the men went for a swim, they looked over my kai room, opened the refrigerator and the food safe, and I think it was the sight of the dry tea and dishcloths hanging on the line—and perhaps my glasses which I polished with care—that made Mrs. Worth cry spontaneously, "Mr. Neale, I'm astounded that *any* man can keep a place as clean and tidy as you do."

When Worth and Taylor returned from the beach I asked them how long they had taken to sail from Papeete.

"We didn't come directly from Papeete," answered Tom, "but from Maupiti." This is a small island a hundred and fifty miles west of Papeete. "It took us seven days."

"Perhaps you'd all like a shower?" I suggested.

"A bath! My God!" cried Tom Worth. "I've been dreaming of a bath for a week."

I had long since rigged up a bucket in the bath-house so that I could sluice water all over myself at the end of each day, and the ladies had the first bath after I had provided them with dry, clean towels.

"You do think of everything, don't you?" said Mrs Worth.

"You're an astounding bloke," said Tom as we sat waiting on the veranda, smoking his cigarettes. "The Consul in Papeete said you were quite a character—but I never thought you'd be quite like this. I don't know—I'd rather expected—"

"A hermit with a long beard?" I laughed.

"In a way—yes." He spoke seriously.

Taylor clipped in, "What staggers *me* is the way you've got everything fixed up. It all looks so easy!"

I recorded every detail I could remember of that

afternoon in my diary and that night I had supper with them on board the *Beyond*, although there was quite a sea running in the lagoon so that I had some difficulty getting alongside in the *Ruptured Duckling*; but once I was on board and Mrs. Worth had gone into the galley to start cooking dinner, Tom brought out a bottle of excellent rum, held it up and said, "How about a drink?"

Now it was ten months since I had tasted alcohol, and never once during that time had I even so much as thought about it. I never miss drinking—but that doesn't mean to say that I don't enjoy a drink or two, particularly rum, and I looked at the bottle in Tom Worth's hand, almost afraid of the effect it might have on me. He must have noticed my hesitation for he refrained from pouring a drink for himself until finally I said, "Thanks! I'd love one."

He poured out a more than generous measure, handed me the glass and asked, "Water?"

Water! No fear! This was much too good to dilute.

We followed the first rum with a second. Cigarettes were handed round. What a wonderful feeling it was, sitting back in the cockpit, yarning, while somebody else cooked my supper! Tom and his friend lost no time in telling me the latest news from the outside world. I remember thinking, doubtless after the second rum, "Neale, are you sure it's really you sitting here?" It all seemed so unreal, so impossible. Only a few hours previously I had been perfectly happy entirely alone on the island—and now here I was, a member of a yachting party. It was too much to take in that first night, and sometimes I could hardly believe I was really there. I might have been watching a film. It didn't seem to be me sitting there, sipping rum. The impact of meeting four strangers after ten months during which I had not spoken to a soul, the excitement of actually talking and listening, was a far more potent intoxicant than the rum.

Suddenly I shivered. I felt quite chilly, for I had rowed out in my singlet and shorts. It must have been the nervous excitement, or perhaps the breeze was stronger a hundred yards out in the lagoon. Tom Worth fetched me a cardigan so that I should be warm enough to enjoy my supper.

I don't suppose I shall ever forget that supper as long as I live. I dare say other people living in conditions of hardship have reached similar conclusions to mine: I had long since accepted my rather monotonous diet as part of life hardly worth a second thought. I had enough to eat and that was what mattered.

But now Mrs. Worth called out cheerfully to her husband from the galley, "Tom! Supper's ready."

We started with vegetable soup, good thick vegetable soup, and then, while we waited for the next course, Tom poured me a glass of ice-cold beer, then his wife handed me a plate of beautifully cooked meat from the *Beyond*'s refrigerator. I remember, too, there was something else I hadn't tasted for a long time—real roast potatoes in thick gravy, and bread thickly spread with tinned butter.

It was not just the change of food I found so exciting; what amazed me was my host's casual attitude to *quantity*. "Would you like some *more* potatoes?"—"Sure you've got enough gravy?" And on top of it here I was eating bread and butter with meat. For a moment I became quite worried lest they run short, forgetting that within a week the *Beyond* would be lying off some port, and Tom Worth would be able to go ashore and in half an hour re-stock his larder. It seemed inconceivable to me and I felt a twinge of guilt as the meat was followed by lavish portions of tinned fruit, with real tinned cream —for once not coconut cream.

My First Visitors

As I rowed back to the shack later that night I found myself, to say the least, slightly happy—in more senses than one.

The following morning, I decided the time had come to reciprocate and entertain my guests to lunch. For though I myself was more than a little bored with island produce, I could well imagine that after seven days at sea, fresh fish or eggs would prove as exciting to my guests as their tinned soup had been to me.

Good fresh fish seemed the answer, especially as the Taylors had asked if they could go fishing. So I went on the reef with them to catch enough lunch for five. I lent them spears but they were unable to catch a single fish. It was almost pathetic to watch their efforts. One forgets how easy fishing becomes when you live in the islands, and I think they were puzzled that I was able to catch six cod and parrot fish and three crayfish in such a short time.

Overhead as we fished the air was alive with birds that seemed to have been drawn to Anchorage from the other motus—perhaps disturbed by the arrival of the *Beyond*. Terns by the hundreds wheeled smoothly in the air, perpetually frightened of the frigate birds—nature's bullies with whom the smaller terns were destined to live from birth to death.

As we slowly walked, searching for fish, towards the north end, we came across rows of frigate birds watching us unblinkingly.

"Ugh! Horrible, revolting creatures," cried Mrs. Taylor, and then asked me, "You must have read Frisbie's *Island of Desire*? Do you remember his description of the frigates?"

She certainly knew her books, for nobody ever described frigate birds better than Frisbie did; how they sat in row upon row, watching Frisbie "with cold objectivity, snobbishly"; ugly, brutal, shiny, black birds with their big red wattles.

"They give me the creeps," added Mrs. Taylor.

"Yes, I remember Frisbie's description," I replied and then surprised *her* by quoting, " 'Eyes red and utterly cruel, birds as emblematic of evil as the raven'."

Back in the shack I cooked the cray, but despite my good intentions, Tom Worth insisted that we lunch on the *Beyond*. I think that Mrs. Worth felt I deserved a day off from housekeeping. Luckily my spring onions were flourishing at this time, so I collected a large bunch and presented them with these, together with a few eggs. These were a great success, and after lunch on board I spent most of the rest of the afternoon yarning and chatting, unashamedly enjoying the opportunity to listen to human voices.

They were due to leave early the next morning for Samoa and Fiji, and I cannot remember feeling any apprehension about their impending departure. Often when I was on my own I had wondered whether I should feel homesick for civilisation once my visitors had gone. I had envisaged a sudden longing, brought on by this unexpected human contact and had even imagined myself begging a passage back to the nearest inhabited island.

None of this happened. From the moment they arrived, it seemed perfectly natural that they should anchor in the lagoon. It seemed natural, too, that we should greet each other in an almost casual way, even though I soon became excited by all they had to tell me. But once it seemed natural for them to arrive, I had to accept the fact that logically it was equally natural that sooner or later they would have to leave. So on this second evening, although I wrote half a dozen letters which they had kindly promised to post, I cannot remember after turning in, feeling really sad at the prospect of their departure.

The following morning, they all rowed ashore for a last bath, and, as I recorded in my journal, "I gave them some more spring onions, eggs, melons, fish, which they said they appreciated very much. They gave me some tea, sugar, a jar of Scotch blackcurrant jelly and a little flour."

And then just before the *Beyond* sailed, with a strong south-easterly wind to blow her on her way, Tom Worth came back to the shack with a final gift—a bottle of rum.

This touched me very much, and as the *Beyond* sailed out towards the pass, I did in actual fact experience a queer feeling of loss. I remember thinking, too, how vastly different their lives were going to be from mine once their pleasant cruise was over. Even when they reached Apia in Samoa there would be bright lights (of a sort), cars, busy streets, cinemas, hotels; so-called luxuries which, however desirable, exacted their own price in tensions, problems, congested humanity.

It was a price I had long ago decided I was not interested in paying. So now I stood by the edge of the old pier watching their sail disappear round the end of the island from whence they would head for the channel and the open sea. It would soon be dusk, the end of another, but this time an unusual, day on my island. So unusual that I watched for a little longer because this had been a happy time. But once the *Beyond* was through the pass and heading out to sea, I turned my back on the lagoon and strode up the coral path to the shack.

The first thing I did was take off my shorts and put on my strip of pareu again.

9. *Down with Fever*

ONCE MY VISITORS were gone and life had resumed
its normal routine, I became involved in a new task which
was to have far-reaching effects on my health. Of course
I never suspected this at the time. But I was preoccupied
with doing something about the one eyesore which spoilt
my beautiful island. This was the remains of the ancient
pier constructed from coral blocks in the old copra days.
In '42 the same hurricane which had caught Frisbie
had wrecked and devastated it. The pier had never been
rebuilt, since copra, having lost its value, was no longer
produced. As a result the wreckage had lain scattered
now for ten or eleven years; a tumbled mass of heavy
blocks just as the hurricane had hurled them all over
the beach that fatal night.

I had been so ashamed of the mess when the Worths
arrived that I felt I had no alternative but to rebuild the
pier and use it for fishing. Had I guessed the amount
of work that was going to be involved—and the time it
would take—I would never have started. But at first,
when I cheerfully began lugging the chunks of coral
into place, the job looked so simple, a matter of a few
weeks at the most.

The original pier must have been about seventy yards
long, stretching right out to the reef. The foundations
were still in place on the fringe reef beneath the shallow
water, but that was literally all, and my "rebuilding"

consisted of lifting, pushing or rolling the irregularly shaped coral stones into the water from the beach or the edge of the undergrowth, where the storm had tossed them, and back on to the foundations. Sometimes I had to prise the large blocks out of the sand and gravel with my pick or crowbar.

By the end of August, although I had been working three hours a day for nearly a month, I seemed to have made no headway. This was not surprising, for, since I had no rope or tackle, it sometimes took me an entire morning to push one coral block along the beach. In order to move others, I would leave them until high tide, as they were lighter to move under water. Often I had to abandon work for several days because the tips of my fingers were raw from the many sharp edges of the coral, which was as difficult to handle as a hedgehog. And as I knew from hard experience, once a scratch became infected, fever might follow within a few hours.

It was a long, tough task. Each time I had trundled half a dozen of these "hedgehog" blocks into position, I had to "pack" them. I remembered reading years ago an article describing the way the Derbyshire men in England build their dry stone walls, and my technique must have been similar. The blocks by themselves looked solid enough, but I knew it was the small stones, laboriously collected on the beach, and then painstakingly pushed into every cranny, like a sort of dry cement, that would give the pier its real strength.

It was hot and dry and beautiful that summer and the days seemed to fly by. There was so much to do. The wild duck had to be looked after, the fowls had to be fed —and that meant hunting for uto. The garden had to be tended and regularly supplied with new topsoil each time a brief storm washed some of it away. Whenever this happened, I would have to get my shovel, row the

Ruptured Duckling to the far end of the island, load her up with dirt and then row back, or sometimes pull her through the shallow water close to the beach, until we arrived opposite the shack, from where I would carry the sacks of dirt to the garden and spread it out—to last until the next storm.

Evening did not bring much rest or repose, for, even if there was nothing else to do, I had to fish for the cats —and this must have become an increasingly annoying chore for I find that about this time I referred frequently in my journal to "caught fish for the damn' cats." Yet I would not have been without them for the world.

I was very contented and happy that summer, for by now the garden was producing a supply of vegetables, and though the stores I had brought from Rarotonga were rapidly diminishing, and I was having to use the same tea five or six times to make it spin out, I had eggs, the weekly rooster, fruit and vegetables, as well as unlimited fish. There seemed no reason not to be happy. True there *was* a great deal of work, for unexpected problems were always arising; a bit of roof would need to be re-thatched; I discovered the kai room floorboards needed replacing; the cook-house walls required strengthening; it was necessary to hack back the dense tropical under-growth which always threatened to crowd the path to the shack out of existence.

All these chores took up a considerable time, but I always found an hour or two to work on the pier each day, though progress in those summer and autumn months was so grindingly slow that sometimes I despaired. Yet, even if I were occasionally tempted to abandon the project, I felt in a curious way that Suvarov had given me so much happiness I owed the island something in return, so that rebuilding the pier became synonymous in my mind with repaying a debt. Perhaps it all seems a little foolish now, looking back, but then—alone and happy and my own master—it was a very real and honest emotion.

There was another reason, I must admit. So far I had succeeded in completing each task I had set out to do. I had rebuilt the cook-house, even made my own new stove. I had repaired the shack, and built a neat path leading up to it. I had built a fowl run, and was getting as many eggs as I needed; I had made a garden out of a wilderness, and the vegetables which grew there now were helping to sustain me. I had even tamed the wild duck. I just could not give up the pier. I wanted to succeed in everything.

I had, however, so far given no thought to one serious problem—my diet. Eggs, fish, coconuts and vegetables seemed more than enough to keep me going in the ordinary way, but three or four hours a day of extra hard physical work on the pier began to make me feel more tired than I had ever felt when doing similar work back in Raro or Moorea. And yet I was not overworking by normal standards—that is, if you apply the standards of a man who fills his belly with at least one good meat meal a day.

But that was just what I was not getting. And, though it took me some time to realise it, this lack eventually made itself plain. For though my actual health remained magnificent, I never seemed to have sufficient energy. Just about this time too, the fowls stopped laying, and for a while I was faced with a shortage of eggs. Nor had I any tomatoes, for though the plants were as tall as I am, the blossom still did not always turn to fruit.

Soon I was forced to begin taking long rests in the middle of the day, something I had never done before in my life. Next I developed an insatiable craving for meat; in other words for the single, solitary tin of bully beef which was now all that was left, but which I was determined to keep for Christmas Day. It sounds ridiculous, but day after day I now had to fight lonely battles over that one tin. I would go into the kai room, look at it greedily, handle it lovingly and say to myself, "Neale, you fool—eat it! For all you know a yacht may come in tomorrow and help you out."

Once I even got out the opener and had almost punctured the top when I suddenly realised that I *had* to keep that one tin for Christmas. It became a point of honour; more, a test of self-discipline. I threw the tin down on the kitchen table, and, like a man who has had a furious quarrel with his wife, stalked out of the shack, and walked up and down the beach in moody, sullen anger until it was dark. And that night, after yet another eal of fish, I wrote in my journal, "Made a fool of myself today. That tin of bully stays unopened till Christmas Day. Will compromise tomorrow with a rooster, but fowls don't seem to satisfy me and I hate the messy business of preparing them." I must have been reading a book by Frisbie that evening, for I find that in my journal I added "I know how hungry Frisbie must have felt when he wrote, 'I would sell my soul for a tin of bully beef, an onion, a cup of tea and a slice of bread plastered with butter and jam!'"

To make matters worse, I was struck down with fever. This proved to be the worst bout so far, and came just at a moment when my resistance was at its lowest. I had been depressed before but this seemed the final straw. The symptoms were unmistakable—chattering teeth, hot flushes (so that I never really knew whether I was hot or cold) and the feeling that my legs were going to buckle under me.

I managed to gather a few drinking nuts around my

bed and lay down to sweat it out for thirty-six hours. Maybe it was lucky I had no idea the bout was going to last for nearly four days.

I hate now to think of the dizzy heights to which my temperature must have soared. Yet the curious thing is that I can remember almost every detail of those four days—and those four never-ending nights.

The fever engulfed me in waves, and looking back, I always associate it with the pounding on the reef and the pier. I suppose it was the only sound I could hear as I unwillingly hovered between moments when my brain was clear and that other semi-delirious dream world which always seemed to be reaching out for me. Each time I felt myself slipping down there, I struggled to hold on to the real world, and as I struggled, the pounding in my head (or out on the reef) would increase, so that it began to seem, in a way, like drowning.

I can remember those fits of fever now (or so I like to think) with a complete, crystal clarity. I can remember being suddenly afraid at the height of one bout that I had forgotten to bury my cache of tools, and managing to struggle out of bed and walk shakily towards the door. (But I begin to wonder now if I really did this, or if it was only a dream so vivid that I really believe it happened.)

The sweating was the worst. I would fall asleep, and then wake to find the bed soaked, and I would congratulate myself that I had at least slept soundly. I felt so alert and fresh whenever I awoke like this that I believed I must have slept for hours. Then I would look at the clock, only to discover that I had been asleep for less than five or ten minutes.

This freshness quickly vanished and soon, as I lay dazed and soaked and shivering on my bed, the dreadful ague would reach out and take me. Every bone in my skinny frame seemed to rattle, and though I would double the blanket and drag it over me, it made no difference, I seemed to shake for hours, and then as it reluctantly relented, a dry throbbing fever took over. My head ached and burned and seemed to swell to such a size that I seemed to live somewhere inside it in my dream world, but couldn't imagine this huge, echoing, throbbing space could possible belong to me.

Looking back, I cannot remember which moment of the fever was the most unbearable. I only know that whichever stage I was passing through seemed the worst. When I was sweating I longed for the ague. When I had the shakes, I would wait almost impatiently for the headache I knew must follow, and when that came and my head felt as though it were going to explode, the only thing I wanted was the intolerable sweating back again.

A period of startling awareness followed each bout. For a time I was suddenly back again in my own little world and vividly conscious of what must be done to safeguard it. The cats had to be fed, uto had to be collected for the fowls, the eggs needed searching out. All these urgent necessities crowded in on me, but there was nothing I could do until the fever passed.

When the fever finally left me after four days and nights, I somehow managed to get up and totter to the edge of the beach, where I lay down in the warm water. Then, as I recorded in my journal, "Felt very weak, but managed to collect some eggs and had ten for tea."

But it was another week before I could gather the strength to work again on the pier.

10. The Pier—and the Great Storm

Despite the setbacks brought about by fever and my lack of meat, slowly, very slowly the pier was beginning to take shape. As the end of the year approached, its completion had become an obsession with me, so that somehow or other I still managed to put in an hour or two each day despite my enforced midday rests which were becoming ever more frequent, for by now I was having to go farther and farther afield in search of small packing stones.

Around November my tobacco ran out. I am not a heavy smoker and had only been smoking one home-made cigarette each evening, and had always kept the butts to re-roll. Nonetheless I was startled at my real sense of dismay when I dug into the tin and found I had only enough to roll one more cigarette.

I smoked it slowly, savouring each puff of the thinly rolled tube, and when I could smoke no more without burning my lips, I stubbed the butt out and emptied the fragments of tobacco back into the tin.

I did not realise immediately how deeply this was to affect me, but the next morning, for the very first time, I suddenly felt desperately lonely. I would have given anything for the sight of a yacht. During the next few days my depression became worse; although the pier was coming on splendidly, I no longer seemed to have the heart to do any more work. And on top of this, my appetite seemed to disappear and for several days I suffered from bad stomach trouble.

I realised now the root cause of all this trouble. Every evening after a dispirited supper, the craving for a smoke became terrible. I had learned to do without meat but somehow no cigarettes drained away all my energy and resolve. I became very thin.

And then a miracle occurred. I was sitting in my office reading Conrad's *The Nigger of the Narcissus* when Mrs. Thievery jumped up on the table, half missed her footing, and in one wild scramble, knocked over a pile of books and magazines I had stacked up neatly against the wall. I cursed her as they fell to the floor. The thud of the falling books made Mrs. Thievery—unused to unexpected noises on Suvarov—jump clean into the air.

"These damned cats!" I growled, and was about to lean down to pick up the books when something stopped me.

There, lying on the table, as though produced from a conjurer's hat, was a packet of cigarettes.

At first I hardly dared to touch it. Then I grabbed the packet, ripped it open and pulled out one of those beautiful, white, smooth cylinders.

Savouring the moment of anticipation in case it vanished before my eyes, I lit up. Then in a glow of relaxation, I recalled that when the *Mahurangi* left, the skipper had given me a few packets of ciagrettes and I had carefully stored them away in my office. One of them must have slipped between the books. If Mrs. Thievery hadn't lost her footing, I might never have found them.

"Had my first cigarette for a month," I wrote in my journal. "It tasted like something out of this world, and feel so much better that I celebrated with six eggs properly fried for dinner, and as a reward gave my companions extra large portions of an eel which I had caught on the reef. All hands very contented tonight but tomorrow will unwrap the 19 cigarettes left and remake them, two out of each one."

Next morning I awoke feeling an entirely different person. One of the first things I did was to break open each cigarette into my tobacco tin so that before long I was able to increase the number to thirty-eight cigarettes sparingly rolled in my own papers. I determined to make them last over a month, and planned to smoke the last one on Christmas Day after I had eaten my bully beef.

Alas, for human intentions. I, who had previously never smoked very much, now entered into a fit of madness and smoked all thirty-eight within five days. I knew it was mad but I could not help it, and after they were gone the craving returned and tortured me far worse than before.

I felt I could do no work. For days I lazed around, waiting, waiting, waiting for Christmas Day—and my tin of bully beef. The craving for cigarettes was bad enough, but now I knew there was not a shred of tobacco on the island some of my longing seemed to become transmitted into a hankering after meat, a slice of bread and butter or, from time to time, a bar of chocolate.

The craving for meat tortured me worst of all. Possibly I was still suffering from a touch of fever, for sometimes I woke in the night sweating with anticipation and, when I had dropped back into disappointed sleep I would dream of home, and my mother lavishly spreading thick hunks of bread with butter. Visions of hoggett, a famous New Zealand meat (half-way between lamb and mutton) invaded my subconscious thoughts, and even after I awoke I seemed to see big pot roasts of hoggett in front of me, at the foot of the bed, or on the shelf where I kept my few books.

And then my dreams took a new and horrifying turn. Until now they had always centred on plain but hugely satisfying dishes. One night, however, there was a startling change. No longer did I crave hoggett, nor even bread and butter; only one mouth-watering dish. There, on a great silver platter with, I remember, a highly ornate carving knife and fork, and surrounded by a mound of exotic vegetables, was the wild duck.

I woke up shivering. The impact was as terrifying as if a head waiter had lifted a silver cover to reveal the elaborately cooked head of my best friend. Even though it was the middle of the night I jumped out of bed and rushed down to the beach to await the dawn and make sure the wild duck was still alive.

How long I had to wait I don't remember, but soon after first light I was relieved to see her flying in. Only then did I go back to bed. I fell asleep instantly and did not wake again until nearly noon.

With the bright sunshine of another beautiful morning the dream receded and became almost ridiculous, and that evening I could laugh at it as I fed the wild duck and she followed me around; indeed, I forgot about it . . . until the dream recurred. And it went on recurring. Night after night, hungry, miserable and fed up with fish, I turned in—and each night there she was, cooked to a turn on a silver salver.

Of course, I was passing through a highly emotional phase at this time—emotional, that is, for a man who rather prides himself on being matter-of-fact. I realise now it was caused by the total lack of tobacco, complicated by my hunger for meat and the rather worrying knowledge that I could no longer stand the taste of fish nor stomach the thought of another rooster.

But dreams have curious repercussions. I began to discover that, having dreamed about this delicious meal night after night (and indeed, this dream plagued me for well over a fortnight), I was now somehow seeing my beloved duck through different eyes. The dream and the reality had somehow treacherously merged. I was horrified to discover that I was now questioning my reluctance even to think about cooking the wild duck. After all, I was desperately in need of a change of diet, so surely there could be nothing wrong in simply ensuring my survival. Perhaps my duck might even feel there was a certain rightness in sacrificing herself to save a friend? Slowly but surely the murderous longing began to suffocate my last remaining scruples, so that when she waddled up to eat out of my hand I found myself thinking how easy it would be to grab her and wring her neck. Surely there was nothing lovable about a slightly ancient and tatty duck? Each evening she came to me, waiting to be killed. I must be mad not to oblige her.

But still I hesitated. It sounds ridiculous now, the inner struggle I endured. I didn't then—I never will—credit birds and animals with human feelings, but somehow that duck seemed to have crept into a rather different category. It was the only living thing which had come to the island and had become a friend during my stay. I had worked for weeks to gain her trust, and now at last she *did* trust me completely. I am not a sentimental man, and don't want to over-dramatise the situation but gradually it was borne in on me that I just couldn't bring myself to betray that trust.

Each day she waddled after me; each day she came to be fed; each evening she flew off to Whale Islet. And still each day these murderous thoughts continued to torment me until one morning the temptation became so great that I almost put a hand around her neck. I was sweating. One twist and she would be ready for the pot. And then she gave one trusting innocent quack. It was enough. My hands fell to my sides.

After this experience, I determined not to feed her by hand again. She came as usual next evening and I laid out her uto and the can of water. But that wasn't her recognised routine any more and so she waited for me to stretch out a handful of food towards her. When I didn't do so, she refused to eat. I didn't like it. I felt bad about her—but I wasn't going to risk her life again.

From that moment on I refused to feed her and she in turn declined to eat. This struggle between us lasted for a week, during which time I felt perhaps at my lowest ebb. Then one day she failed to fly in.

I waited until noon, but when there was no sign of her I almost panicked. Without hesitation I pushed the *Ruptured Duckling* out into the midst of a rough chop and rowed over to Whale Islet. I thought she might be hurt, but there was no sign of her there either. I searched the motu from one end to the other. She had gone, and I never saw her again.

I must confess that after this my life seemed to become infinitely stale and dreary. I must have been feeling very low and disconsolate for there are gaps in my journal right up until Christmas Eve. But on this day everything changed with one amazing stroke of good fortune. I discovered a turtle on the beach.

It was the first time I had seen one since I landed on Suvarov over a year previously, and as she made her painfully slow way along the beach, I could see that she was enormous, and must have weighed three hundred pounds. I ran towards her—for here was the meat for which I longed so desperately—but I had great difficulty in turning her over on to her back which was at least three feet broad. But having done this—and it's the only way to make a turtle helpless—I was not certain about the next step. For despite all my years in the islands, I had never seen a turtle killed.

I touched the underneath of the thick, leathery neck and she immediately withdrew her head close to the shell. After some thought I returned to the shack, and collected my hammer. Then I went back to the beach and gave the turtle one terrific blow on the head. It seemed to kill her, for her head and neck relaxed, which enabled me to cut off her head—a hateful, difficult job. But as I worked, cutting through the leathery skin and panting with exhaustion in the hot sun beating down on the beach, I kept on saying, "Neale, this is meat—you've got to do it if you want to keep going."

There was no shade and it took me over a couple of hours, using my sharpest knife, to cut off the giant shell. When I had prised off the shell, I found that some of the meat was greenish in colour, some red. I knew that natives eat the green meat, but hungry though I was, I couldn't face it.

So I cut away the red meat which looked just like beef, and heaped it up to carry back to my larder. After cleaning the shell, which I kept, I buried everything else, including the green meat and the intestines, in the sand.

I celebrated Christmas Day with an outsized turtle steak—it seemed the finest meat dish I had ever tasted—and because I was afraid the rest would go bad, I cut it up into chunks and stewed it with some spring onions. After this feast I decided to keep my last tin of bully beef for New Year's Eve—by which time I reckoned the turtle would be finished.

That one week of good eating worked wonders. With plenty of good, nourishing turtle meals each day, I discovered that not only my health but my whole outlook was taking a turn for the better. I am certain the meat helped to cure my craving for cigarettes, for suddenly everything looked brighter. Indeed, I felt so much better that I (almost) forgot I had no tobacco. My loneliness and depression vanished and I even forgot about the wild duck. Starting on New Year's Day, I began to work five hours each day again on the pier. And I found myself tackling this work in a totally different frame of mind, for now the blocks I had piled up stretching out from the beach no longer struck me as a pathetic monument to a task whose vast scope had hitherto simply mocked my puny efforts.

Well fed, cheerful, and full of new heart, those same blocks of coral now looked a remarkable—even magnificent—achievement, whose completion only needed one last spurt of effort.

It took me six weeks of hard labour, but in the end I had the pier completed. Every block was in place, every niche had been carefully packed. By the middle of February I had not only rebuilt the famous pier of Anchorage—having rolled, carried or trundled every single stone of it myself—but at the far end I had also built a small platform with a thatched roof which would be cosy for fishing on nights when the weather was bad.

I surveyed my handiwork with considerable pride. It looked solid enough. For I had—often with great difficulty—placed the blocks dead square on the natural foundations of the fringe reef so that the top of the pier was almost as smooth as a paved road, with every crack between the differently shaped blocks carefully packed with smaller stones or even gravel from the beach. I could walk on it without rubber shoes.

It had taken over six months to build and suddenly as I looked at it, I remembered when I had first decided to work on it. It was the day the *Beyond* had sailed out of the lagoon. And as soon as she left for Apia I had hauled my first block of coral into position.

Six months! As I walked along the pier, testing my weight, looking for any loose cracks, I was thinking what an eventful period it had been—fever, hunger, tobacco craving, even the strange episode of the wild duck. And yet, despite all the problems, the pier was finished.

Now the strain and the sweat were ended, and when I stepped back on the beach and looked at the pier from a distance, I reflected that in New Zealand a gang of men, armed with a block and tackle or bulldozer, would have charged a small fortune to build it. I could hardly believe my temerity in starting such an enormous task single-handed. Six long, hard months. And yet it seemed as though it was only yesterday when Tom Worth had presented me with the farewell bottle of rum, and I had thought how shabby the pier looked.

A celebration of some sort was needed, so when I had secured the last piece of coconut thatch on the roof of my new fishing hut, I declared a holiday to commemorate the official opening. I must have had a touch of the sun that day for I described a long imaginative scene in my journal.

"Amidst scenes of great enthusiasm the new wharf was officially opened by the president of the island council, Mr. Tom-Tom. The trans-lagoon vessel *Ruptured Duckling* berthed at the end of the wharf while the band played, 'Oh, for a Slice of Bread and Cheese!'

"In his speech, Mr. Tom-Tom paid tribute to the contractor and his staff, who in the face of numerous difficulties successfully completed the colossal undertaking. He went on to say that with the great depth of twelve inches at the end of the wharf at low tide, the largest vessel could now berth with safety and that in the future we could hope to see many more vessels use this port.

"Afternoon tea was served by Mrs. Thievery and her able assistants. In the evening a dance was held at the pavilion after a fine supper of fish guts and rats' tails. Young Mr. Sparrow occasioned much amusement by his humorous song 'Uto for Breakfast, Uto for Lunch.' Dancing continued until the small hours and was concluded by the singing of the Suvarov national anthem, 'We Ain't Had a Ship in Years'."

Well, I had done it. It had been a near thing and once the task had nearly beaten me. But in the end I had succeeded in completing what I had set out to do—and that pleased me very much.

I was only just in time. Within twenty-four hours of our "public holiday" the barometer started falling with alarming speed. Though the next morning dawned perfectly calm, the flat, still sea was the colour of lead, and Anchorage was blanketed by a stifling, suffocating heat. Nothing moved—not a palm frond, not a spiky pandanus leaf—and when I walked over to the east coast and looked out from Pylades Bay to the sea beyond the reef, even its calm held the hidden menace of a disguise, as though it were hoping to trap the unwary by its seemingly placid surface.

I knew the portents only too well (that trite old phrase about the calm before the storm) and strode back to the shack. There was no immediate hurry—but equally there was no doubt that serious trouble was on the way. Before doing anything else, I checked my survival cache of tools, making sure my extra matches in their sealed tin were dry, and then took the box over to the "burial hole" in the outhouse. Next I lit a good fire on my brick hearth, and while it was burning, went out with my spear for a concentrated hour of fishing. It seemed provident to lay in some emergency rations, for there was no telling with a big storm; it could last a few hours or a few days.

I had plenty of cooked uto, but I foraged around for a couple of dozen more, which I cooked, and then I laid out double rations for the fowls. Next—as the first puffs of wind ruffled the palms—I inspected the garden for any ripe fruit which would be mercilessly blown off the plants when the inevitable storm broke.

By noon the calm had given way to the white horses that caused Conrad to write that the whole sea resembled " a floor of foaming crests" and the palm fronds were no longer still. The first winds had reached Anchorage, after travelling hundreds of miles from some great storm far away to the north. By the time I had tested the wire guy-ropes lashing down my shack, I felt there was nothing more I could do in the way of preparation.

A dozen or more ku wrapped in breadfruit leaves were slowly baking on the hearth. A couple of reef cod were in the stewpot. I had sufficient uto to withstand a siege of several days—and in a way it *was* rather like preparing for a siege against an implacable foe. In the outhouse I had a plentiful supply of wood, and in the kai room a good stock of arrowroot, plenty of fresh vegetables including yams, cucumbers, tomatoes, spinach and onions. A dozen drinking nuts, a couple of ripe breadfruit and a stem of bananas completed my emergency rations.

By mid-afternoon gigantic seas were visible breaking all along the reef to the north, and before sunset, when the storm was beginning to reach its height, seas more huge than I had ever seen before began breaking right across the half-mile width of the entrance to the passage. The rolling mass of water surged on through and over the passage, only gradually losing its massive force as it lost impetus in the great stretch of water inside the lagoon.

I remember saying to myself, "Neale! This could be another 'forty-two."

The wind had now risen in tremendous force, and the last thing I did outside before seeking the sanctuary of my shack was to struggle a couple of hundred yards to the highest point of the island. This was only fifteen feet above normal sea-level, but already from my vantage point it seemed as though Anchorage was beginning to shrink as waves came rolling through the gap in the barrier reef to engulf the beaches and creep up more and more greedily every minute. Just behind the beach and not far from the pier the first coconut tree fell with a crash, torn out by the roots, as though giant fingers were already starting to loot the island. Waves pounded right over the pier and as I looked north, I could see more gigantic waves tearing through the half-mile stretch of fringing reef separating Anchorage from Whale Islet, surging into the lagoon, by now rapidly becoming an immense waste of boiling seas.

For a few minutes more I stood clinging to one of the five tamanu trees. I don't think I was physically frightened; I was more fascinated, even overawed by the inevitability of it all, by the relentless march forward of the seas until the beach seemed to vanish before my eyes, and the white foam of the waves boomed and crashed into the very jungle itself, then trickled out over the roots of trees like soapy water, only to be met by the next great wave. Anchorage seemed so puny, so fragile against this steam-roller; yes, that was the word Frisbie had used, "Anchorage is damn' fragile"; and as I stood there, soaked and blinded with a mixture of salt spray and the rain already starting to pelt down, I could understand another of Frisbie's descriptions of the wind "shrieking", for this is what it actually did. It shrieked through the palm fronds with an almost animal wail.

For a few moments I stood watching, fascinated, listening as the noise was punctuated by the crash of another big tree falling.

There was nothing I could do. Somehow I struggled back to the shack, fighting my way across the yard, already littered with the smashed branches of trees. When I reached the veranda and opened the door to my office, the wind in a sudden burst of ferocity caught it, almost dragging me back, so that I had to struggle to get inside.

I managed to slam the door and secure it. I had already battened down all the shutters, but the wind threw itself against the tiny shack with such malevolent fury that it seemed it was deliberately trying to tear it from its flimsy foundations. The shack suddenly seemed filled with draughts; the doors and shutters rattled angrily; for the first time I realised I was cold and stiff. My limbs ached with the effort of reaching the shack, and when I lit the lantern—for the shuttered room was in darkness—and caught a glimpse of myself in the mirror on the bedroom wall I hardly recognised my own face, bright red and still glistening from the wind and the sting of the spray and rain. I rubbed myself down briskly before making a cup of tea.

Though it was not, of course, blowing so hard as when Frisbie had been caught on the island, the storm was spectacular enough for me. More coconut palms were falling, nuts started flying through the air, and the tin roof vibrated like a buzz-saw.

For it was the *sound* of the storm that was so incredible. I had weathered many a storm at sea, but there the sounds had been different and I had grown accustomed to them, but now the only resemblance to the wind whistling through the rigging came when the guy ropes twanged with each sudden gust. The wind was so strong that it blotted out almost all other sounds, though every now and then, I could hear the crash of another tree falling. At any moment I expected the roof of the shack to be torn away. (It certainly would have been had it not been for the guy ropes.) As the night wore on, coconuts falling on the roof were to make sleep virtually impossible, and though I made another cup of tea before turning in, I was almost afraid to remain too long in the cook-house which was more flimsily built than the shack.

For hours I stayed sleepless, almost deafened by the storm, keeping my lamp burning all night, since I didn't want the roof crashing in on me in the dark, but the wind attacked each shutter crack with such persistence that it gave only a miserable light and there was no possibility of reading. All I could do was sit on the edge of the bed, tensed and waiting.

Sometime during the night I must have dozed off, for without warning the biggest crash of all seemed to burst almost on top of me. I ran to the office door, stumbling over a heap of paperback books strewn all over the floor. Wrenching at the door, I tried to push it open against the howling wind. It refused to budge. I put my shoulder to it and pushed with all my strength. Still I could not move it. This was no wind wedging the door against me —and yet the shack seemed secure. I could tell that because of the steady hammering of rain on the tin roof. Only now did I realise what had happened—the veranda roof must have gone.

I lit the hurricane lamp, managed to open one of the shutters, and clambered through on to what was left of the veranda, dreading what I would find. Heavy rain hit me in the face and in a second I was drenched, but I remember that, even before I looked around me, I realised that the wind had eased a bit, and I could tell immediately that it had backed to the north-west. That,

The Pier—and the Great Storm

I knew, meant that the worst of the storm was over.

No wonder I had not been able to force open the office door. One end of the veranda roof, and the strong pole supporting it, had crashed down. But thank God the kai room was safe. When the coast-watchers had enclosed one end of the veranda, they must have reinforced it, but that part of the veranda roof thatched by the natives from the *Mahurangi* had been torn away.

Beaten by a pitiless rain, I stumbled through the wreckage. It would take weeks to mend the veranda but there was nothing to do now except scramble back into the shack and close the shutter behind me.

In the office I put the books back on the shelf, and then looked at the barometer. It had started to go up. As I returned to my bedroom and extinguished the hurricane lamp, the distant thunder which had growled for hours came closer and burst directly overhead. Almost continuous lightning seemed to penetrate every crack in the house. Within a few moments the original rhythm of rain drumming on the roof seemed to change; now sheets of rain came down, solid sheets.

The storm was nearly spent. I heaved a sigh of relief and went to bed, first yelling into the night, "Go on Huey! Bang those drums!" The cats curled up at my feet and I slept fitfully.

Next morning I woke to discover the sun bursting through a tracery of the palms just as though nothing eventful had happened. It felt good to be alive. I must have slept late for the cats were demanding food.

I got up, stretched, then walked outside—and stopped in utter dismay. Four old trees had crashed across the yard. Half the fowl-run fence looked as though it had been torn up by a giant's fingers. One banana tree had been uprooted, the roots sticking into the air. I could have kicked over the garden fence without any effort.

Miraculously, the shed and bath house were still standing, but the veranda was a wreck.

Piles of brushwood, blown from other parts of the island, had turned the place into a mess where before I had prided myself on keeping it spick and span. I could have cried.

There was little I could do immediately, however, and so I walked down the coral path, fighting my way through a tangle of smashed branches and uprooted trees, and often being forced to climb over scores of palm fronds snapped off like cotton threads. Finally I reached the beach.

My pier was gone. I just stood and stared. Six months of backbreaking labour had vanished in six hours. The massive blocks which had torn my hands and fingers and brought me so much fever had been hurled back in chaos towards the beach, and now lay more or less all jumbled up where I had found them.

One glance was enough to explain how it had happened. It had not been the heavy seas bursting through the pass which had demolished the whole wharf (for these had simply gone cascading on into the centre of the lagoon before spending themselves). The gap between Whale Islet and the northern tip of Anchorage provided the answer. For through that mill-race thousands of tons of water had been hurled straight at the pier.

"I was so downhearted," I wrote in my journal, "that I didn't even use any bad language, but walked slowly back to the house."

11. *Saved by a Miracle*

Over three months had passed since the great storm. Six weeks or more had been required to repair the damage and clean up the mess, though I never again attempted to rebuild the pier.

On this Saturday morning—it was May 22, 1954—I had seldom felt better in my life. The hurricane season was now behind me, having left hardly another storm worth noting in my journal, and now calm weather had arrived and the garden had never looked or yielded better. For once there was hardly a real care to worry me. Everything was perfect. It was a beautiful morning with not a thing to warn me that within a couple of hours I should be virtually paralysed, and trembling with fear and in agonising pain.

I had made a good breakfast off some ku which I had left overnight wrapped in leaves to cook on the hot bricks, fed the cats, and after washing up the dishes, I pushed the *Ruptured Duckling* into the lagoon and started to row her over to One Tree Island where I had decided to plant a few sprouting coconuts.

This coconut planting had recently developed into a sort of hobby. It started almost by accident when, on an easy day with no uto or firewood to collect, I suddenly fancied a change of scenery and rowed over to one of the motus. I had picked a fine day, but subconsciously I suppose I needed to persuade myself there was a reason for going. Coconut planting seemed the perfect answer, and in an odd way this pastime soon gave me an extraordinary sense of achievement, because every time I did it I had a feeling I was cheating evolution by a hundred years.

On this particular morning I took my time rowing across the lagoon. I remember there was a slight headwind and that I reached the motu by seven a.m., pulled my unwieldy boat almost up to the edge of the coral beach, and without thinking lifted out the iron weight which served as my anchor and hurled it on to the beach.

Then it happened. A searing sensation shot across my back and as I doubled up in agony, I cried out in sudden pain.

At that first moment on the beach I was more astonished than frightened. I kept absolutely still, the sweat running down my body. Then I gingerly tried to move—and cried out aloud involuntarily, as the pain seemed to lock me into immobility. I waited—it might have been a few minutes, but I have no recollection of how long I stood there. I do remember I was trembling all over. When I stood still I felt no pain, but the instant I tried to move, the smallest action sent spasms galloping through every muscle.

I was in no doubt as to what must have happened. I was certain I had dislocated my back, and remember telling myself, "Neale, if you give in, this is the end."

By now the early morning haze had lifted, and already the sun was beating down harshly on my bare and ruined back. From where I crouched I could see the palm tree skyline of Anchorage shimmering across the lagoon. Because of the water, the distance looked deceptively close—hardly more than a quarter of a mile away. Yet in reality the flimsy shelter of my shack was over three miles away, and in my crippled state I was horribly aware that the chances of getting back there were infinitely remote. Nor did I even think I could possibly make the ten yards to the *Ruptured Duckling*.

I could see her floating in shallow water, and because I knew I had somehow to reach her, made an effort, but could not even turn in her direction. The pain was so intense at the slightest movement that it literally made me sweat all over. I could turn my head—but nothing more. Now that I think back, the curious thing was that I, who was normally able to bear pain, did not *dare* to invite even a brief spasm of pain by any movement. And yet I could not stand there like a lonely statue until I dropped of fatigue.

At last I decided to try and reach the boat on all fours. I let myself subside gently on to the beach near the anchor weight, and crouched there gasping until a little strength returned. Somehow I regained a touch of confidence, but I did not dare to lie down (though I longed to ease myself into a more bearable position) since I was only too well aware that once down there I would never be able to get up again on my own. As a result, I simply stayed where I was, crouching in the hot sun for what must have been the best part of an hour, trying to summon sufficient courage to make a move. I almost tried several times, but at the last moment instinct, or terror of the pain I knew any movement must bring, stopped me. I just could not face it. As the moments dragged on, sweat streamed off me as though I had stepped out of my bucket shower.

I find it impossible now to describe how, or exactly why, I brought myself to make a final effort. I was horribly, almost petrifyingly aware of the desperate fix I was in. Here I was, virtually paralysed, two hundred miles away from the nearest human being. Nor was there any reason why a boat should unexpectedly call at

Suvarov. Entirely alone, I would die on One Tree like a dog, gasping in the sun, unless I made some supreme effort to help myself. At this moment, it struck me I was probably likely to die anyway, but looking back on that moment now, I am sure that what fired me into agonising effort was not so much an instinctive sense of self-preservation, as a desperate craving to reach my shack. It was my only home and I *had* to reach it. And even if I were doomed to die in total isolation, at least it would be on my own bed. This longing to reach Anchorage, this overwhelming instinct to be on my own island, gathered such strength in my mind that at last I made one supreme effort. It was incredibly difficult, and I must have made a dozen false starts; stopping and sweating profusely each time as though a powerful hand were preventing me from moving. Since then I've heard that a man with a stiff neck is totally unable to force himself to turn his head suddenly. This was my predicament, complicated almost beyond endurance since my whole body seemed clamped in one vast, torturing vice.

I still do not know how I did it. I simply cannot recall exactly how I summoned the energy and determination which enabled me to crawl the ten yards to the boat. I have no idea how long it took, because each crab-like movement forward brought on an excruciating pain which necessitated a pause to stop and rest. But somehow, through a haze of pain, crawling and slithering in the warm, shallow water, I managed to reach her. And curiously enough, when I did and had half-raised myself to grab the gunwale, the pain decreased. It was as though the act of clutching at solid support, even the reassuring familiar sway of the *Ruptured Duckling*, induced some mental balm.

I rested on the thwart, gasping and endeavouring to keep as still as possible, feeling terribly lonely and help-

less. Months ago back in Raro I had never envisaged a
moment like this, never dreamt that a single, unthinking
action could plunge me into a situation where even the
natural instinct to hope seemed presumptuous. For—
sweating and gasping, hardly daring to breathe—it
wasn't this moment of pathetic achievement which
worried me, it wasn't even the pain. What stared me
unblinkingly in the face was the bleak, hopeless future.
For what chance had I to survive? How could I feed
myself unless I could move about? Such thoughts,
whose frightening implications were hardly crystallising
clearly in my pain-dulled brain, were still infinitely more
disturbing than the physical pain. Often before on the
island I had felt lonely or even physically low. Fever
had left me like a dish-rag, but at least once I had pulled
out of it, I had never been helpless. Now for the first time
I was facing the one situation I had never imagined
possible; the moment when I found myself forced to
admit, "Neale, now there's *nothing* you can do."

That moment was on me. And I was down to the
last and only refuge I had—which was to reach Anchorage, even if I died in the attempt. Fortunately, on my
way over I had not unfurled the sails since I had faced a
headwind when coming over to One Tree Island. I
reckoned I could count on the breeze and current to help
me drift back. But first I had to clamber aboard.

The slow crab-crawl across the beach had exhausted
me, but half-lying, half-crouching there, I sensed that the
only way to get into the boat was a painful progression
through small stages.

Eventually I managed to stand upright, though I was
so terrified of moving my back that I stayed in one
position for about ten minutes. Then I gingerly lifted
one leg from the knee. Providing I didn't twist my
pelvis, it didn't hurt too much. I tried the other leg—

successfully. Inch by inch I turned my feet, edging round, until I faced the boat. The sweat poured down me, off my head and into my eyes. I couldn't even lift an arm to wipe it away.

After a short rest I lifted one leg again, bending the knee until I could just about step over the side of the *Duckling*. The slight movement of the water made it tricky, but I managed to inch one leg over, and then the other. After that I carefully lowered myself on to the seat, sitting stiffly upright.

Once I was there, the pain seemed a little less agonising; or, maybe, as one gradually comes to recognise in life, the human body has a capacity for coming to terms with suffering. Fortunately I had left my machete in the boat and I had a long painter, so I was able to gather up some of the rope into a sort of coil in front of me, and then with one agonising swipe I managed to cut through the nearest section and so free the anchor. Almost immediately I could feel the *Duckling* beginning to drift away from the beach.

Looking back, I must have spent the next four hours in a daze of pain. Somehow or other, with the wind behind me, the *Duckling* started to make erratic progress back towards the island.

I cannot tell the story of that frightful trip in detail, nor even coherently, for the simple reason that I can only recall it in an episodic sort of fashion. I remember I had to sit bolt upright; it was the only safe way. The sun, which I normally regarded as an ally, now seemed to have become my most pitiless enemy, because at the moment of clambering into the boat, my hat had fallen off, and I could not reach it—nor, had I been able to do so, could I have placed it on my head.

Fortunately, I was able to move my arms backwards and forwards—so long as I did not raise them, or move my back. So, by sitting as still as possible, I slowly inched my hands towards the two oars, and managed to get them into position. I was facing the way we were going and did not have the courage to try and turn round, but I was able, from time to time, to make short "reverse" strokes, in the way a boatman can push a boat while facing his objective. They helped to keep the *Duckling* on a fairly straight course.

Ahead of me I could see Anchorage, and without doubt the most agonising thing of all was the manner in which the island seemed so tantalisingly close, yet frustratingly never seemed to come any nearer. I realised, for the first time in my life, what men dying of thirst must feel at the sight of a mirage. The island looked close enough for a couple of puffs of wind to carry the *Duckling* on to the beach. I could clearly see the palms moving—the palms that Stevenson described as the "giraffe of vegetables"—yet an hour later, two hours later, the skyline seemed just as near—and just as distant. Every instinct told me that I *must* be moving towards her, yet at times my dulled mind refused to accept the truth, and I would sit, the sun beating down on a head that was normally covered, terrified to make a false movement, and wonder if, in fact, I *was* really making for Anchorage. I almost gave up hope so many times. The hours of agony seemed interminable. The shimmer and sheen of the water dancing in front of me seemed to cause yet another pain that bored into my eyes and brain.

Once or twice I made a false movement. Then, after painfully righting myself, I could do nothing for a few moments except sit still and upright, sweating and trembling with the memory of the sudden, jerking pain.

At last I arrived off the beach, moving in very, very slowly, and now I suddenly became desperately preoccupied with how I was going to beach the boat. Looking back, I think I must have now decided that life was worth living, or maybe the pain was a little more bearable, for I no longer felt quite so lonely and helpless. I was nearly home—but I was terrified at the prospect of not being able to beach the *Duckling*. Although the anchor had vanished when I had cut the painter to get free from One Tree Island, there was still a considerable length of rope left in the bottom of the boat. This rope was in every sense literally my last sheet anchor. And it worried me into a state of impotent frenzy. On the one hand, I certainly did not possess the strength to use it to drag the boat up the beach. On the other, I dare not lose hold of it, because otherwise I would lose the boat, and without her life on the island would be virtually impossible.

I am still hazy about what actually happened, but through my clouded memory I recall the whole problem being solved by a providential wave, which hit us without warning. All I remember is a sensation of being lifted, I lost my balance and yelped with the sudden stab of pain. When I opened my eyes, the *Ruptured Duckling* was aground on the edge of the beach, so close to my boxwood chair that I might have placed her there myself. She had half keeled over so that I was able to roll out of her, crawl up the beach with the severed rope and tie her to the nearest palm.

It was now midday, and a fierce and uncompromising sun made me painfully aware I must reach the shelter of my shack as quickly as I could. After a brief rest, I managed to regain my crab-crawl position, and started to make my way up the coral path towards the front porch.

Only a confused recollection remains of the ensuing moments of that journey. I presume my slow and agonising progress must have been stretched over a very long time, but I know that at last I managed to roll into my bed, taking with me two coconuts which I discovered in the kitchen, a glass, a machete and my home-made calendar.

I remember I knew I simply *had* to have the calendar, because it had suddenly become more important to me than food and drink. Living entirely alone tends to make one highly aware of all the awful things which can descend on one when one is helpless, and now a sudden fear had gripped me—that I might be doomed to lie in bed, eventually recover, and yet remain entirely ignorant of how many days, or weeks, or even months had passed. It would be like losing one's whole grip on time, like having part of one's life irretrievably lost. As I rolled on to the bed, clutching my paper calendar pad, I remember thinking that as my clock was working, and I would be bound to wake from time to time, I would then be able to mark my calendar as the days passed. This marking of the calendar was to become a complete and consuming obsession.

I must already have begun to calculate—or perhaps dream is a better description of my state at that moment —that I was somehow or other bound to recover in the course of a week or so, and already this comforting prospect had become so confused with the real state of affairs that it seemed quite natural for me to envisage lying on my back for weeks, without even bothering to wonder how I would be able to exist without food and water. I was so relieved and so happy, just being on my own bed with the cats purring close at hand, that I never somehow gave a thought to such vital necessities as food and drink. I remember one mundane thought, however. As I lay there, groaning, I recollect thinking I would give everything in the world—yes, even the

Ruptured Duckling—for a cigarette. Just one cigarette, or if that were asking too much, then just one stub which would be sufficient for a couple of whiffs.

I must have dozed off from time to time, for I can remember almost nothing of the days and nights that followed. Strangely enough I have no recollection of opening my drinking nuts, though later my rescuers were to discover they had been opened and the glass had been used (as I planned) to prevent me wetting the bed.

But the possibility of rescue never for a moment entered my mind. The chance was too remote and absurd. I would just have to stick it out and hope the jammed muscles would unlock. That was as near to a miracle as I could expect.

I remember I could roll my head and move my arms, so I suppose I must have held up the nuts while lying on my back, and clumsily opened them with my machete. When I wanted to urinate I used the glass, then emptied it on the floor. But all this I was to learn later from my rescuers who arrived with such miraculous timing that, if this were a work of fiction, I would be blamed for contriving the clumsiest of long-armed coincidences. And I must admit that even now, when I think back, it all seems to have been too ridiculously "pat," as though I were guilty of exaggeration; and then I turn to the book *Man and his Island* which one of my rescuers wrote about his trip in the South Pacific, and there in black and white is the chapter describing what happened.

I don't suppose I shall ever forget that day. I was awake, lying on my back, when I distinctly thought I heard voices, a sort of low hum like two men talking. Not being a religious man, I hadn't thought much about miracles and at first I imagined it must be a dream. And, of course, it *had* to be a dream, however real the voices

sounded, because the only other alternative must be that
I was going mad. I opened my eyes. Every object in
my bedroom became clearly visible. Then I heard the
voices again, followed by footsteps—and suddenly,
wildly excited, I knew that this was no dream and that
those voices must belong to fishermen who had landed
on the island from Manihiki. I tried to shout, but though
I could feel the muscles moving in my throat, no sound
came out.

The voices suddenly changed from a low incompre-
hensible jumble of sound into a distinct clear cough—
the sort of apologetic cough a man makes when he enters
a room unbidden—followed by two simple words, start-
lingly clear:

"Anybody home?"

"Who is it?" I managed to croak.

"Two fellows off a boat," cried the unknown voice.

"Come in, come in," I gasped.

In retrospect the delicacy displayed by my unknown
visitors over entering my bedroom seems almost ludi-
crous. Two men now entered the room. My field of
vision was limited, because I was unable to lift my
head, but I was relieved to see quite clearly two brown,
bearded faces—brown, yet the sunburned brown of
white men. They stared at my face for a moment, and I
noticed their eyes travel down to my chest, my pareu
covering my loins. Then, in a surprised voice, one of
them said, "Christ! He's a white man!"

"My name's Tom Neale," I gasped again. "Dislocated my back. You'll have to help me up. What day
is it?"

"Wednesday." They were still staring at me.

"What's the date?" I asked.

"The twenty-sixth."

I still couldn't believe it. "I must have been lying

here four days," I said. "Trying to summon the nerve to sit up."

"Good God!" The stranger nearest to me looked really concerned. "You must be starved. What can I cook you?"

"I sure would like a cup of tea, thanks." (Later they told me I even managed to grin.)

"Where shall I brew it?" he asked, glancing round my simple room.

I told him he could make a fire out in the cook-house, and this amazing man (whose name I was very soon to discover was Peb) briskly told his friend, "Go and make some tea, Bob, and I'll see if I can manoeuvre him into a sitting position."

From his accent I had already guessed he was an American, and as he bent over me now, his black beard brushing my face, I recognised the type—enormously strong, an inborn longing for adventure, undoubtedly a good sailor, all these obvious qualities concealing an inner capacity for gentleness and kindness.

"Don't worry, Tom," he told me as he slid one strong arm under my shoulders, "it'll hurt once—but only once."

It hurt like hell, but now it hardly seemed to matter. I gritted my teeth and in one movement he had me sitting up. As he had said, once it was over, it was over.

"It's made you sweat," he said gently. "Here, let me help you." He vanished into the kai room, came back with a teacloth and began to wipe the sweat off my back and shoulders.

"I'll be all right in a minute," I said. I could hear his companion calling from the cook-house that the fire was going.

"What you need," replied Peb, "is a good meal. Every single rib you've got is showing. Hang on for a little while. I'll row back to my boat for some supplies."

Then, almost as an afterthought, "Do you use cigarettes?"

There was nothing I craved more in the world, but somehow that American accent with its curious expression, "Do you *use* cigarettes?" coming on top of the shock of relief and the certainty I was not dreaming, produced a ridiculous reaction. I started laughing. I don't really know why, but I think I must suddenly have remembered a Western I had read one evening in the shack. Sitting alone, I'd laughed then over a line when someone posed a question to the sheriff, and he had replied, "You're darned well right I do." I had an uncontrollable impulse to answer Peb with the same phrase until I saw the concern on his face. "You all right, Tom?" he asked anxiously.

"A smoke would be really something now," I compromised.

That night I ate my finest meal for many a month—a bowl of good thick vegetable soup, a tin of meat and some tinned fruit. There were other miraculous things which Peb had brought over from his yacht. A stiff tot of rum—my first drink since I had finished the bottle Tom Worth had given me—a carton of cigarettes and, almost more important, a bottle of liniment with which my two new friends took it in turn to massage my back.

That massage did me a world of good, so much so that by that evening I was even able to sit up on one of my box chairs—so long as I remained bolt upright—whilst Peb and Bob told me the story of how it was they had come to arrive on Suvarov at such an amazing and providential moment.

"Peb" was the nickname for James Rockefeller. He lived in Maine, and had come to the Pacific some months ago in his boat, the *Mandalay*, accompanied by his friend Bob Grant. They had spent the time sailing from island to island, "Which," as Peb explained, "is the perfect way to learn about the South Pacific."

Peb was making notes and taking photographs for a book—which he was later to publish—and I have the impression that they had enough money to last them for some months. Over the years I had met several young, adventurous Americans who had saved hard, then thrown up their jobs to make a trip of this sort before settling down, and they fitted into the mould.

Having left Tahiti nearly eight hundred miles astern, they had set course for Samoa when Peb, who had been looking through the *Pilot Directions* had come across what he described to me as "one magic phrase." It was: "Suvarov is uninhabited."

They decided to spend a couple of weeks on a desert island.

"As soon as I read the word 'Suvarov' I remembered all about the place," Peb told me that evening. "I'd read how treasure had been found on the island, and of course I'd read my Frisbie before I left the States. When I glanced through *Pilot Directions* I just felt an impelling urge to see what it was like."

Not for a moment had it ever entered their heads there might be someone living on the island. Peb told me they had both stared unsuspectingly at the deserted beach through their binoculars until something suddenly riveted their attention. It was my boat pulled up on the sand and, next to it under the palms, my special chair.

They anchored and rowed ashore. "One of the things that struck us was that the name '*Ruptured Duckling*' had been painted on your boat with a very shaky hand," said Peb. Once on the beach they discovered the path I had made and walked up it towards the shack. It must have been an eerie sensation—the *Ruptured Duckling*, the chair—and yet no sign of life. "It reminded me a bit of the *Marie Celeste*," Bob told me.

On reaching the porch, they had both shouted loudly. But although their voices must have been forceful enough to have been heard all over Anchorage, there had been nothing but a strange, uncanny silence.

There seemed nothing to do but go inside the shack.

"The first room I looked into seemed to be a sort of study or office," Peb told me. "I could see books on the shelves and the desk piled high with papers and magazines. Then I looked into the second room—your bedroom. It was a bit dark and at first I couldn't see anything except the lower end of your wooden bed with its white sheet; then by God, I saw two feet on that sheet. We were so astounded that Bob whispered to me that we ought to have knocked, and he coughed, hoping you might hear us. I had a horrible fear that a dead man lay in that room. It was then that I called out, 'Anybody home?' Boy! Was I glad when I heard your voice!"

My visitors stayed two weeks with me on Suvarov, nursing me back to life with wonderful care and gentleness and building me up with good solid tinned food from the *Mandalay*. It was the sort of food I had not eaten for months, and it was borne in on me once again that the human body needs meat of some sort to sustain it, especially when there is heavy manual labour to be done. Swapping our food worked very well, for they were delighted to eat fresh fish, eggs, fowls, vegetables and fruit, while I wallowed in tinned pork and beef, and cooked wonderful fresh bread with their flour.

In those two very happy weeks, my back seemed to improve with an almost incredible speed, though, as I noted in my journal, I was unable to use both hands to wash my face until June 8—nearly two weeks after the seizure. Twice a day Peb or Bob rubbed me down with liniment and soon I was able to walk fairly easily and even take an occasional dip in Pylades Bay. Every now and then, however, a twinge doubled me up as it stabbed its way right across my back, and reminded me vividly that things were far from right just yet. Although each spasm passed comparatively quickly, it was clear there was some lasting damage.

"Don't think you've licked it," Peb told me towards the end of their stay. "You'll never lick it till you see a doc."

Not unnaturally, I had been giving a great deal of thought to the future, for I was really frightened about the state of my back. The memory of that morning on One Tree motu still disturbed me as vividly as the occasional twinge of pain, and I knew Peb was right. I would never recover until I had some sort of medical attention. I might be able to carry on for a few months if I were careful, but what sort of a life would it be for a man hundreds of miles from any sort of help, perpetually forced to walk gingerly, think twice before daring to lift a spade or chop down a nut? I was in no doubt now that it was exertion that brought on the crippling pain; a sudden jerk, the quick instinctive tensing of muscles, even before the message had passed from brain to limb. A disability like this was obviously an impossibility on an island where physical effort was vital in order to keep alive. I had to face it. This serious weakness would not only make life impossible, but little short of suicidal into the bargain.

Had I had a companion, a Man Friday, I might have been tempted to remain, for Peb's constant help had proved that a companion could quickly get me into a sitting position, and unlock the muscles I would have been powerless to free alone. But there was no companion, and soon even Peb would be on his way.

"I suppose I'll have to leave," I remember saying as we walked slowly along the beach just as dusk was falling, the time of the day I like best of all. "I hate the idea, but I'm scared of my back—and I want to live a little longer."

Peb was sympathy itself. Tactfully he offered me passage to Pago Pago although he did not have much room on the *Mandalay*. I refused, however, for two reasons. Were he to land me in Samoa, I would be left with no prospect but to borrow or work for the money necessary for a passage back to Raro on the infrequent boats that plied between that port and Pago Pago. If I *had* to return to Raro, then I wanted to go there directly. And secondly, something else held me back, something that inhibited me from travelling away from my island with Peb and Bob, wonderful fellows though they were. They could never grasp just what leaving the island was going to mean to me. There was no reason why these two young, intelligent men "doing" the Pacific should understand. I admired their courage and eagerness to discover what life was like amongst the islands in the real tough way (rather than on a conducted tour), but I knew too that for them the experience would never have any deeper significance than a wonderful interlude; a nostalgic memory related around the fireside to their children, brought alive with albums of photos so that they could relive the great adventure of their youth.

To me, in sharp contrast, the island was *not* an adventure, it was something infinitely bigger . . . a whole way of life; and so, if I had to leave Suvarov, I knew it was vital I should spend my last few weeks alone on the island. I have seldom ever felt anything more strongly and I think Peb understood this, for he did

not attempt to persuade me to change my mind, but
merely nodded at my attempt to explain my feeling, and
agreed to my suggestion that when he reached Pago Pago
he should send a cable to the Commissioner in Raro,
telling him I was ill, and asking him to instruct the next
schooner for Manihiki to pick me up on her way back.
The Commissioner would probably be angry since this
sort of thing cost Government money, but in my present
mood I was not unduly over-sensitive over the risk of
incurring a little official wrath.

And so on our our last night together we had a farewell
party, and I cannot do better than quote from my journal
of Sunday, June 6: "Killed another rooster for the last
meal my friends will share with me here, since they are
due to leave tomorrow provided the weather is suitable.
We had a wonderful meal with a bottle of champagne
(chilled in a wet bag hung in the shade in the breeze) and
finishing off with chocolate cake (iced and cooked on the
boat) and some good coffee. The best meal I've yet had
here."

After our meal, a tot or two of rum kept us yarning half-
way through the night which was clear and filled with
stars. I was very moved because I liked these two boys
immensely, and could not escape a gentle melancholy
(eased by the rum) knowing that, life being what it is,
this was probably the last time I would ever see and
talk to the two men whom chance had sent to save my
life.

Just as I anticipated that night, I never have seen Peb
or Bob again, though we have corresponded, and I hear
Peb has married and settled down.

The morning of their departure, Peb asked me over to
the *Mandalay* and there, ready for me, were some stores,
a good supply of cigarettes, and a couple of bottles of
rum.

"They'll tide you over until the island schooner come to pick you up—" Peb gave me a final handshake— "and for God's sake be careful."

"See you one of these days!" cried Bob, and then in no time, it seemed, Bob was winding up the anchor and almost before I realised what was happening, the *Mandalay* was slowly moving as the first wind caught her sail. I stood by the broken-down pier for a long time watching her slowly getting smaller.

When the yacht was almost out of sight, I turned and walked up the coral-edged path to the shack and brewed myself a cup of tea. It was an important moment. During the last two weeks the three of us had proved conclusively that three can be good company. Never for one moment had we exchanged a cross word, never experienced a moment of discord. They had proved staunch friends, the sort of friends one does not often meet in a lifetime. Yet when the kettle started to hiss, and I warmed the pot, and put a larger spoonful in for good luck, I felt an overwhelming sense of peace.

Two weeks were to elapse before the ship called to pick me up.

Looking back, although I had to be very careful about moving around and was always conscious of my back, these were the happiest weeks of my life.

12. Farewell to the Island

Long before I could set eyes on her, I knew it must be the Manihiki schooner. That smudge dusting the horizon where the sea met the sky could only mark her arrival, for no other schooner would be so far off the trade routes. And though I had been anxiously scanning the horizon for days, worried about my back, a sudden thought now hit me like a blow between the eyes, a truth I had stubbornly refused to admit until now. Within a few hours I was going to be aboard that schooner. And once there I might never see Suvarov again.

I can never forget that moment. I sat down on my beach chair to steady myself, and sliced open a drinking nut as I watched the sail take shape. An emotion closely bordering on panic was taking hold of me; not only apprehension at having to meet the people on the schooner, nor even the prospect of enduring a life I disliked in Raro. It was something much more profoundly disturbing than that. I just didn't want to leave. I knew, with a dull feeling of despair, that the last thing I ever wanted to do in life was to leave. Mr. Tom-Tom came out of the coconut palms and leapt as lightly as a coiled spring on to my lap. As I automatically stroked him I realised, as I had never realised before, that I had never wanted anything more from life than moments such as these.

The impact of seeing that tiny smudge, the realisation

that there was now no way of postponing my departure, brought a sudden forlorn portent of loneliness welling up in my mind.

The urge to stay became so strong that the most ridiculous subterfuges flashed through my mind. Perhaps I could hide! If the landing party failed to find me, they might presume I had died on another motu, and so go away and leave me in peace. There might even be time to sail to another motu and hide there. I wondered (only for a moment, though) if I could stage my "death" —by leaving a few clothes on the beach as though I had been drowned.

Once pain recedes, one forgets it so readily, and as I sat there I was assuring myself that even though the back pains did return, I would be tough enough to survive.

They did not seem too bad now, but, as I sat there, gingerly shifting round, I remembered with an illuminating flash of clarity that brought me right back to reality something Peb had said to me as we sat drinking rum on the porch one evening: "It's one thing to be killed or drowned in a hurricane or storm—in a way, it's a sort of end that'd suit you, Tom. But it's something else to lie on your back, unable to move, all alone, slowly starving to death, alive but paralysed, knowing there's more food than you can eat just ten yards away."

He was right, of course. There was no escape. With a sigh I rose and stretched, tumbling a protesting Mr. Tom-Tom on to the beach.

There was still a little while left before the ship reached the shore. During those moments I walked back to the shack and started to pack my old battered leather suitcase, putting in the clothes I had not worn for eighteen months, two or three shirts, my "best" shoes. I kept out my only pair of respectable shorts and one shirt. I would dress up in these in the last few minutes. But before that

I wanted to wash up for the last time, in the kitchen I had virtually created myself.

I spent a little while there and was careful to leave everything spick and span, for sooner or later a yachtsman would pass this way. Then I went for a last look round my garden, so spruce now, and so different from the wilderness it had been before I had killed all the wild pigs. The tomato plants came almost level with my head. Involuntarily I started to hack back some of the Indian spinach with my machete. Then I suddenly stopped, blinking in the sun. Why bother? The whole garden would be suffocated in less than a month.

I went on to the chicken-run, opened the door and made it fast. The roosters and hens must run wild now, for without me and my familiar dinner gong they would starve. Like me, they didn't appear anxious to abandon their home, but stayed inside the confines of the wire door just scratching around, whilst I collected seven eggs. I thought I would give these to the captain of the schooner; fresh eggs always make a welcome change at sea. On a last impulse I caught and tied up four of the fattest clucking hens which might just as well go to the captain too. They wouldn't be of value to anybody now, running wild on Suvarov.

I got out the cats' box which I had kept, for I had known I'd never leave them alone. They would be snug enough in that during the trip back to Raro. If I let them loose on the schooner, I would probably never see them again. Some people hate cats and I could remember seeing a man throw one overboard in a fit of rage.

I was packed and ready long before the ship came through the pass, for I knew from experience that when vessels deviate to lonely atolls, they do not like to linger. As she came slowly into the lagoon I recognised her. She was an ugly 300-ton twin-screwed boat called the *Rannah*, and I felt a pang of disappointment, for I suppose I had been hoping that it might have been Andy in the *Tiare Taporo*. It would have helped a lot to see Andy at this moment of my life.

By the time the anchor chain had rattled down, I had carried my suitcase, Gladstone, my tools, the fowls and the cats' box down to the pier, and I stood there, watching as the ship's boat was lowered to pick me up.

Then a couple of Cook Islanders splashed ashore and greeted me cheerfully. I knew them, for both had served with me on other vessels. I tried to be polite, but I could not force the words as I climbed carefully into the boat and sat there, upright, while two men rowed me to the schooner.

I had a bit of a job getting aboard, for the *Rannah*, which carried a crew of twelve and half a dozen cabin passengers (plus innumerable deck passengers!) rode high in the water. But everybody seemed anxious to help, and then I saw the skipper, John Blakelock, an old friend, giving me a welcoming wave from the top deck.

Blakelock must have been in his fifties, a powerfully built man who had seen the world—in all sorts of jobs. He had been policeman, planter, trader, as well as sailor.

I waved back as best I could, but I don't know whether he saw me, for like everybody else he was in a hurry. Everybody seemed in a bewildering rush, and in a few moments we were moving again, and I was leaning over the *Rannah*'s stern watching the atoll recede into the blue-grey distance.

It was June 24, 1954. One or two passengers came up to me, and tentatively started asking questions; but

I didn't feel like talking. It was one thing to talk to chance visitors to Suvarov, but that was very different from being accosted by strangers who did not even bother to introduce themselves, but were patently only anxious to be able to tell their families they had actually met and spoken with a crazy hermit who had been living on a desert island.

My daydreaming was rudely shattered by John Blakelock's voice behind me, crying, "Come on down, Tom, and let's have a shot!"

I know he meant it kindly, but how was he to tell, how could he realise, that this was the one moment in my life when I most wanted to be alone.

I am not ashamed to admit there were tears in my eyes as the smudge that had been my home for twenty-one months grew smaller and smaller, paler and paler, until finally it merged into the horizon and I could see it no more. Vainly I tried to shut my ears to the jarring sounds around me; the native passengers laughing and giggling, the shouts of the crew, with an occasional expletive thrown in for good measure.

I thought back to the happy evenings I had spent on the beach with the cats purring as the sun went down, to the undisturbed rhythm of a life that none of these people around me could ever remotely imagine, to the day I caulked the boat, the evening I made the candles, the morning I discovered the brick.

And now it was all gone, receding into a sort of dream as rapidly as the island had receded before my eyes. I remember standing there, and suddenly shivering as the captain yelled again for me to join him in a drink. It was not the cold that caused the shiver, but the sudden recollection of an old Tahitian proverb I had heard years ago: "The coral waxes, the palm grows, but man departs."

Part Three

CIVILISATION
AGAIN

13. Six Frustrating Years

Six years lay ahead before I was to see Suvarov again, and frankly I cannot look back on that time without the most wretched memories of a continual frustration, knowing that it was only a bare five hundred miles away.

For Suvarov *was* now permanently out of reach. The authorities made no bones about it. Obviously they didn't relish the idea of my ever returning and did everything humanly possible to ensure that I had no chance to make the attempt. It was not that they were unpleasant—almost the contrary—but very soon it was evident that for one reason or another there was no question of them allowing me to return. Had I been a rich man, able to afford my own yacht, they could not have stopped my going, but since the only way I could hope to return was by diverting a schooner, they held the whip hand. Even before going to plead my case with Mr. Nevill, the Resident Commissioner in Rarotonga—who knew me well—I had taken the precaution of having an X-ray taken of my back at the local hospital. A couple of days later the doctor showed me the plates and assured me in a hearty voice, "There's no evidence of a displaced or slipped disc. It looks more like an acute attack of arthritis." Stubbing with one finger at the indecipherable black and white shadows, he added, "You see—it's here where there's a little roughage."

I stared respectfully at the plates and asked whether any further treatment was necessary. "No, Tom," he told me, "you're quite all right, but for God's sake don't lift anything heavy."

Fortified with this heartening news, I hurried to the Resident Commissioner's office, which was situated just behind Main Street. I found the door already half open, and through it I caught a glimpse of Mr. Nevill. I knew that he must have seen me too, for he called out, "Come on in, Tom."

Few men could have been more naturally pleasant, easy-going and well-disposed towards me than Mr. Nevill. Hitherto we had always greeted each other familiarly in the street, for in a small place like Raro, formalities were reduced to a minimum. He was sitting now in shirt sleeves at his desk as I entered and stood in front of him, awkwardly fingering my hat of plaited coconut.

"I imagine you know, Mr. Nevill, what I've come to see you about?"

"Suvarov, I suppose?" He gave an almost imperceptible sigh. Looking me straight in the face, he came right out with it. "No, Tom—I'm afraid it's not on."

"But why not?" I said desperately. "I don't want to go back straight away—but provided I work hard for a few months—earn enough money to buy some supplies —why *shouldn't* I go? I've proved I can make a go of it, haven't I?"

He was silent for perhaps half a minute, and then in a very quiet but friendly voice said, "All you've proved Tom, is that, but for a miracle, you'd be dead by now."

"But I'm *not* dead!"

"Believe me, Tom, I know how you feel, but I represent the Government and Governments have responsibilities.

And Governments don't rely on miracles, you know. If they did, they'd be in a pretty awful mess."

Instinctively I liked Mr. Nevill. There was no more point in talking. We just shook hands, but as I reached the door, I could not resist saying, "I'm going to write to the Minister of Island Territories in Wellington and put my case to them."

That nice Mr. Nevill had all the answers. In a quiet voice, but still smiling, he replied, "Write if you like, but of course, Tom, you must know that he'll only refer it back to me."

I did write, but Mr. Nevill was right, for when the reply came it was in the negative and dictated to me straight from Nevill's office. Obviously my letter had landed back on his desk annotated with the directive "Do as you think best."

And now the whole machine came into action—a machine that resolutely set the seal on my ever slipping away; for after all it was very simple to stop me. All that was necessary was to warn the local inter-island traders like Dick Brown or Andy that were they to give me a passage to Suvarov the Resident Commissioner would have no alternative but to order them from time to time to put in there at their own expense to make sure I was in good health. Since the island schooners rarely passed by Suvarov, nothing could have been more effective, for putting into Suvarov cost money, quite a lot of money, and what skipper was likely to take this burden on his shoulders?

Only one hope remained—a private yacht; but even here there were snags. Raro, unlike Tahiti, was not a tourist centre, so there was no stream of pleasure boats—and even if there had been, where was I likely to discover one to accommodate my own skinny figure and all the stores I would need?

Time after time I returned to plead with Mr. Nevill.
Invariably the answer was the same and I was forced to
retreat from his whitewashed office shaking my head and
muttering to myself, "Neale, there *must* be a way!"

Of course there was—but it was to take me six years
to discover it.

Meantime I had to eat, so before long I was forced to
take a job as storeman with the Cook Islands Trading
Company—the same firm for whom I had worked before
in the outer islands. The pay was £25 a month. Inevitably, I loathed every minute, for after Suvarov, it
was no easy job adjusting myself, and every moment in
the warehouse found me nostalgically comparing this
dreary commercial existence with the free and intensely
satisfying life I had known on the island.

I found myself constantly irritated. During the past
twenty-one months almost the only time I had ever used
a clock had been for cooking uto; now my entire day
seemed doomed to be governed by the ticking of this
infernal machine. For nearly two years my only clothing
had been a strip of pareu; now long trousers encased and
imprisoned my reluctant legs. Every time I drew breath
I felt choked with petrol fumes from the cars outside my
office window at the filling station. Only occasionally
was I to find something that reminded me of Suvarov. I
had found a place to live and batch for ten shillings a
week, and my new dwelling was almost on the water's
edge outside the town. When the wind was in the right
quarter, I could hear the boom of the reef; whilst nearby,
from the field framed by mountains where my neighbour
kept fowls, I was still awakened each morning by cock-
crow.

Yet I mustn't give the impression that my life in Raro
was nothing but a long and melancholy interlude; nor
that I went to and from my daily work with a face so

miserable that people shunned me. I had friends, I had plenty of work to do, and of course I would often go for days without thinking about Suvarov.

Raro looked much the same. Main Street was just as dusty as it had been before I went away, the Residency seemed just as solid. A new garage had sprung up beside Avatiu harbour, and on the edge of Avarua village there was now a new general store. I found that the radio station near the airstrip had been enlarged, while the sanatorium by Black Rock on the West Coast had been modernised. But basically the place remained just the same—an easy-going, small community clustered close to the bountiful ocean which washed the beaches, and backed by the 2,000-foot-high dramatic peak of Te Manga, the island's largest volcanic mountain.

Before long, despite my restiveness, I began to settle in. Nor did I resent the hard life of a storekeeper. Every morning at seven I collected the keys from the manager's house before opening up the store. My own tiny office, which was in a corner of a warehouse, reminded me in a way of my little study on Suvarov. Its furniture was sparse—only a table and chair—but there any resemblance ended, for when I hurried to open the shutter each morning, I looked out not on a coral path lined with coconut trees leading down to a beach, but on a petrol station by the edge of an unpaved road, so dusty that it had to be hosed down each day throughout the dry season.

I would gaze out on this rather depressing scene for a few moments before picking up my heavy bunch of keys and setting off to unlock each of the warehouses grouped near the store which, in common with all island stores, stocked pretty well everything.

The store where I worked was not only a retail store catering for the Rarotongans, but also the central distributing depot for all the small island stores which the company owned and in which I had worked for so many years. Each of the big warehouses which I unlocked every morning contained bulk stocks, and I was more concerned with this end of the business than with selling in the store, for I had to keep a check on the stocks—which would range from cabin bread filling one warehouse to tinned goods stocked in another—and I also had to arrange for casual labour when a new shipment of goods required speedy unloading. We had a timber yard, a filling station, a paint shop—in fact everything, which at least ensured that my work was not monotonous.

At week-ends I would collect my bicycle and try to work the perpetual feeling of despondency out of my bones by riding right round the twenty miles of coast road which ringed the island. Somehow the exercise always made me feel better.

And then of course there was Andy. Whenever he was back from a trip I used to cycle out seven miles to see him at his fifty-acre plantation.

No one knew better than Andy how I would have liked to return—but he was unable to hold out much hope. Even now I can recall his words to me one sultry evening as we sat on his veranda while his wife was cooking in the house.

I remember that night extraordinarily clearly. I can even visualise the veranda now, with its big tamanu table which Andy had had specially made. We were sitting on the cushions of the bench-type seats where Frisbie and I had often talked, leaning our elbows on this very table. Tonight it bore a bottle of whisky and some water in a chatty.

Andy loved this veranda because, like so many sailors, he took especial pleasure in looking out over his garden with its sloping, well-trimmed lawn which led down to the road. It had a path too, bordered with African daisies, roses and a multitude of flowers set out in pots, backed with hibiscus shrubs with yellow, white, red and even violet blossoms.

I remember staring at him across the table and asking, "What do you think my chances are for getting back to Suvarov?"

He sipped his whisky before replying. Then he said, "Tom, I don't believe the authorities will *ever* let you go back."

Although I had half known this all along, his words seemed loaded with a terrible finality. I knew now that authority had set its face implacably against me. And yet even despite this knowledge, some instinct bore me up because I *knew* that somehow or other I would make it in the end.

At this time one of my few friends was Ron Powell whose boatyard was only a short distance from my shack, and I had fallen into the habit of dropping in on him during the long evenings to watch him building his latest order. I have always admired boat builders, but what drew me specially to Ron was the fact that he had visited Suvarov. Of course we naturally chatted about the island and I made no bones about my wish to get back. Then one evening out of the blue he suggested, "Let's build a twelve-footer for when you go back to Suvarov!"

"You really mean it?" I asked incredulously.

"Of course I do." His pleasant cheerful face was beaming. "You can take your time—there's plenty of room in the yard. Come on, Tom, we might as well get down to some scale plans."

Now, I am no boat builder, but during the next few evenings I hurried straight from the store to Ron's home where we worked until the late hours drawing plans to scale. This would not, of course, be a boat to *take* me to Suvarov, but a boat to use when I *got* there, and I knew just what I wanted. She had to be light and strong with practically no keel and a slight "V" bottom—light so I could handle her myself, haul her up on the beach, turn her over for painting; strong because I wanted her not only for shallow water, but to cross the eight miles of the lagoon.

It was a great moment when those plans were finished. On paper, she was to be twelve feet overall, with eighteen inches of freeboard, a four-foot-six-inch beam, with a centreboard. The mast would be just under twelve feet so that I could stow it away in the boat when I wanted to row.

"When are we going to start building her?" I cried, for the sight of those plans had brought a new purpose into my life. It was a beginning; a token, call it what you will. I knew that somehow the building of that boat would bring me a step closer to Suvarov.

Ron looked at me indulgently and replied, "You can come to my yard whenever you like. I reckon the time that would suit you best is after you've knocked off work."

And so I started to build my boat.

I never looked back, but I never seemed to have enough time. Building a boat demands skill and patience, indeed all one's energy and concentration. Night after night, after a full day's work in the store, I would hurry through my domestic chores and then head down for the yard. But progress seemed infuriatingly slow until I had a stroke of luck.

It was over a year since my mother had died, and now that her estate was finally wound up, I found myself the unexpected possessor of two hundred and forty pounds.

The next day I gave in my notice at the store.

Six Frustrating Years

I know it sounds impulsive to chuck away a job, however dull, but "security" in the islands hasn't the same compulsive value that seems to have been put upon it in the West. If anything went wrong there were always plenty of jobs of one kind or another I could take, and since my outgoings seldom rose over a pound a week, my windfall made me financially secure for several years ahead. Besides, I was obsessed with getting on with the boat, whose progress had somehow become inextricably identified with my chances of returning to the atoll. I had begun to believe that I *couldn't* go back without that boat, and that once it was built everything else would somehow fall naturally into place. Although it didn't eventually work out quite like that, the one driving thought uppermost in my mind was to get her built as quickly as possible.

In actual fact, it was to take me a year, and I riveted every one of the hundreds of nails myself. Even when she was starting to take shape I did not christen her—and I vowed I was never going to launch her until I was ready to take her to Suvarov. Even when she was finished, friends used to say to me, "Hey, Tom! Why don't you put your boat in the water?" Invariably I evaded such questions with the laconic comment, "Conditions for sailing in Rarotonga aren't suitable." I never told a soul the *real* reason, preferring to keep her behind my shack where I erected a frame covered with sheets of roofing iron to keep the rain off.

As the years passed, however, she and I seemed fated to stay on Raro for ever and I almost began to forget how I had connected her building with my dream of getting away. Sometimes now I was almost frightened at the realisation of how swiftly the years *were* passing, how inevitably I was getting older. But my boring, if tranquil, life seemed to act like an anaesthetic until, suddenly one night, talking to Andy about the old days, I was startled into reality by an earnestness in his voice I had never known before. Leaning across the table, he urged me "Give it up, Tom! Do you realise it's five years since you left Suvarov?"

His words brought me right up against the truth. It *was* five years! And I was getting on for sixty!

That night I went home to my little shack and looked around despondently at the things I had been collecting against the day of my return. Already twenty cases or packages were stacked against the walls—ready for the day. There were all sorts of new things I had bought— an emery wheel which I hadn't been able to afford on my first trip, a carpenter's plane, two more saws, a couple of rolls of wire netting, several lengths of twelve-by-one boards for shelving or making tables. I had even bought a galvanised bath tub.

As I made myself a cup of tea I wondered gloomily if it were all worthwhile. Was I—close on sixty—an ageing idiot pursuing an ideal which had long ago quietly and silently slipped out of my reach? Why didn't I face the truth and settle for the sort of life that seemed to satisfy other people? Even Andy—Andy of all people—had said "Give it up!"

Had it not been for an American called Loren Smith who sailed into Rarotonga I think I might have entirely lost heart.

But Smith, who luckily for me decided to stay awhile, was destined to bring me the order of release which I had almost ceased to believe would ever come.

Loren (or "Smithy" as I called him) was about sixty, a cheerful gregarious character who loved the islands, and was perfectly content sailing from one to another, taking a job when he ran out of money. Although he owned a thirty-foot boat of the type known as a Tahiti ketch, which was called *Tahiti*, she had not been built there. He decided to settle down for a spell and work at our local garage. As a result we met quite often, and one day he asked me if I would help him haul his boat out of the water since he wanted to repaint her. As we had no slipway at Rarotonga the job involved using a block and tackle, to say nothing of the P.W.D. bulldozer.

Naturally, I gave him a hand and even helped with the painting as well. Once the job was over and we had put the *Tahiti* back in the water, I got into the habit of visiting Smithy on his boat in the evenings for a yarn. Inevitably, I must have talked about Suvarov. Indeed I harped on my experiences there so often that I was half afraid I had bored him, until one night when we were having a final drink in his cabin, Smithy turned to me without warning, and said, "Tom, if you *really* want to go, I'll take you back there."

I almost dropped my glass as I swallowed the wrong way and choked.

"Tom, I *mean* it," he added.

I was so taken aback that at first I could not reply, but when I did, I forced myself, despite a mounting surge of excitement, to remain severely practical—deliberately, for I didn't want this hallucination to get out of hand.

"That's a wonderful offer," I said as evenly as I could, "but you know, Smithy, you could never get all my stuff aboard."

"That's easy," said this remarkable man as he filled up my glass, "we'll just have to make two trips."

Even now I refused to allow myself to believe him.

"But you've got a dinghy on deck." I must have sounded as though I were *trying* to find excuses. "You could never get my boat on board as well."

"That's okay—" there was not a moment of hesitation —"we'll tow her."

Now for the first time I allowed myself to believe that I might *really* be going back.

It never entered my head to inquire why he had made this generous offer, I just took it for granted, though now, looking back, I imagine it was probably because he wanted to repay me for the work I had done on his boat. That and the fact that he had a natural love of adventure.

We talked long into the night. By the time I went back to my shack I knew not only that this was *real*, but that we were *actually* due to sail within the next three weeks. The very next day I started to send all my packages by lorry to a friend who lived opposite the *Tahiti's* moorings, and who had an empty shed. From then on every evening found me storing some of my stores aboard.

Once again I made the round of the stores I had made so many years before in search of bulk provisions; but this time, although I bought very much the same sort of supplies, my improved finances enabled me to buy in much larger quantities. I had learned many lessons during my first stay on the island, and I was determined not to forget them each time I visited the stores. Above all I remembered how I had needed meat, so this time I bought three times as much bully beef as I had done the first time. I also invested in a larger supply of tea and powdered milk, for I knew how miserable I could be without my evening cup of tea on the beach.

I still had all my crockery and kitchenware; most of my tools were in excellent condition, especially as I had added to them over the years, but on the first trip I had sadly missed garden tools, so now I bought a good rake, a big fork and spade and a wheelbarrow for the topsoil I knew I would have to collect to make a new garden. Since I knew every corner of each warehouse in the

Cook Islands Trading Company, I was able to "scrounge" all sorts of invaluable extras. When I bought my garden tools the manager threw in a tin of fertiliser. Everybody seemed determined to help. One of the men in the paint shop brought me a selection of brushes as a gift just because I casually mentioned how I had had to make my own on Suvarov. One other thing I remembered— to buy half a dozen small children's paintbrushes to pollinate my tomato blossoms.

The news of my departure was, of course, soon known to everybody in Raro, and once again, in those three weeks of rush and bustle, I sensed in the kindness which every-body showed me a trace of wistful envy, as though they would have given anything to be setting off on a similar adventure.

Indeed, I was in Donald's one day buying a couple of old sugar sacks when one of the assistants I had known for years suddenly looked me straight in the eyes, and blurted out, "Tom—will you take me along with you?"

He was a freckle-faced man of about forty-five—young compared with me. There was an almost pathetic eager-ness in his voice, and I suddenly realised that he had been serving behind that same counter even before I left on my first trip. Poor devil!

But it was impossible, and there was only one reply I could make. "I'm sorry," I said, and I really meant it for he was a nice fellow, "It wouldn't work, Jim. Believe me, it wouldn't. I'm going back to Suvarov because I like being alone—and if we were cooped up there together we'd be fighting like cat and dog after a month."

I only needed one companion on the island—a cat. Mrs. Thievery and Mr. Tom-Tom had long since faded out of my life, and had been replaced by another female. (Like my boat she as yet possessed no name. I seemed during this period to have given up using names!) I decided against taking the cat until my second trip, but I did plan to take two roosters and six fowls with me. As there was no room on deck for the crate I had built for them, I decided to stow this in the stern of my boat which we would tow up on the first trip and leave on the island whilst we returned for the rest of my belongings.

Only one thing was really worrying me now—how I was going to be able to pay for my passage. I knew Smithy was not a rich man, and I felt that it was too much to ask him to foot the bill for fuel for his auxiliary engine for two trips of five hundred and thirteen miles each way—over two thousand miles in all.

So, a few days before I had finished loading my first lot of cases on board, I went to Smithy and handed him a bundle of notes—fifty pounds.

"What's this for?" He looked astonished.

"That's for taking me to Suvarov," I replied.

He looked at it in silence for a moment. Then without a word, he stowed the money away. We never referred to the matter again, but I felt much better for having paid my way.

One more call remained to be made—Mr. Nevill, the Resident Commissioner. I knew he must be aware of my plans, but nonetheless, I felt I should go and face him, and tell him as man to man, because despite all the times when he had refused to help me, he had always behaved perfectly correctly, so that we had remained on the sort of terms which never excluded a friendly chat when we met. I didn't want him to think that I was sneaking off behind his back.

I might have guessed his reaction when I went up to his office in the Residency a few days before sailing.

"Mr. Nevill," I told him, "I'm going to Suvarov."

He smiled. "Oh yes, Tom, I know you're leaving."

Then, since this was no longer his official business, he turned to me, held out a hand, gripped mine, and said, "Good luck, Tom!"

On the last night before sailing I made the rounds of my few close friends to say good-bye, wondering, now that I was nearly sixty, how many of them I would ever see again. Andy happened to be in port, so I cycled out to have a final drink with him, and as he sat opposite me across the table, with a bottle of rum between us, he uttered one sentence which I must admit gave me great pleasure, "You never give up, do you, Tom?" This oldest of friends looked almost puzzled. "I wish I knew what it is that drives you to love Suvarov so much."

"I don't know myself, Andy," I admitted. "Perhaps it's just as well that I don't."

I cycled back to the shack and went to see Ron Powell, whose encouragement in building the boat had made me promise that he should be there when finally, after all these years, we launched her. Together we carried her down to the water's edge and then, for the first time, I took her out. She behaved beautifully, as though responding to the knowledge that I, who was now sailing her, had built her from the word go.

We had to have another drink to celebrate the launching, and then Smithy joined us, and one or two others, and we sat yarning until it was nearly dawn.

It seemed as if half Raro had come to bid me farewell on that day in early March, 1960, when we finally sailed. Curious, and I dare say fascinated, people lined the quay. Old acquaintances came to shake my hand and wish me luck. Somebody brought me a pound of tea. A lady who lived in a big house not far from my shack brought a cake she had baked herself. And almost at the last moment before we sailed, the friend with whom I had parked my bicycle came running down to the quay, almost out of breath, waving what looked like a thin black stick.

It was my bicycle pump!

"You found it useful last time," he gasped. "I thought you might need it again!"

Then we cast off, and soon we were sliding out of the harbour. Behind us, Rarotonga slowly grew smaller. First the people vanished, then the bright white houses, then the church, and finally, only old Te Manga stood out starkly against the skyline. Despite my excitement and anticipation, I had a lump in my throat. Wasn't it ridiculous, I thought, how you long to get away from friends, and then it hurts when you finally do.

"Hey, Tom!" Smithy interrupted my daydreams, "Take the tiller while I go check on the motor."

No more time for thinking. We were on the way— back to the island of desire.

14. Return to Suvarov

WE TOOK ELEVEN days to reach Suvarov. We experienced constantly dirty weather with headwinds and sometimes even cross seas running. Despite these drawbacks, however, I managed to scramble into the dinghy each morning and evening to feed and water my fowls and bale out the rain water. I was only able to get in by hauling on the tow line until the dinghy was close up to our stern and then Smithy would hold it whilst I clambered precariously across. It wasn't easy, and when the weather was really bad there was no alternative but to make the passage four times a day to bale her out and stop her from sinking. On one occasion I missed my footing while clambering aboard and fell into the sea, but managed to grab the tow line.

It could hardly be described as a pleasure cruise, for it took all our effort to keep the *Tahiti* on course; we had little time for cooking, and—as far as I was concerned— very little time to think of what lay ahead. The fact that I had been able to return to Suvarov was one of the great triumphs of my modest life, and should have filled me with excitement; yet, because of the bad weather, the voyage of the *Tahiti* was something of an anti-climax. We were too occupied to think. Even eating a cold meal was hazardous when the weather was at its vilest.

The day before we reached Suvarov, the wind dropped, and we spent the night some miles outside the reef. Even though it was a long way off, I could occasionally hear its booming, and I sat on deck—just as I had sat on the deck of Andy's *Tiare Taporo* that night so many years ago—at last able to luxuriate in anticipation, knowing that my island was only a few miles away, and that on the morrow I should be walking along its firm, white beach listening to the lap of the warm waves and the rustle of the palm fronds.

Smithy was asleep in the cabin but now, with the bad weather behind us, I sat under a sky crowded with stars. Only the gentle slap of water against wood disturbed the night. Though we were both dog-tired after the trip, I couldn't bear the thought of wasting this night in sleeping, for it was, I think, the most perfect night I can remember, the sort of beautiful night that must have inspired Masefield's line "The lonely sea and the sky." It all seemed one, as though I were alone in the centre of a vast black sphere.

It was four a.m. before I finally turned in, and I awoke two hours later as fresh as a daisy to a fine sunny morning. Now that there was no wind, we used the auxiliary engine to approach the island, and by eight o'clock we had reached the passage in the reef and Suvarov was there before me.

What a moment to remember! Seen from the deck of the *Tahiti*, nothing seemed to have changed (though I was under no illusions about the mess I would find when we landed). The morning sunlight seemed to catch the tops of the old, eighty-foot palms in such a way that they stood out almost in silhouette—jet black with a dazzling light shining through them. It seemed to me (perhaps understandably!) that the island had never looked more beautiful, and as we rounded the south end into the lagoon I noticed first the canopy of shorter palms that bent almost protectively over the beach, like a natural umbrella, and then the old pier which looked much as it had when I left. Frisbie's five big tamanu trees were still standing—nothing could ever dislodge them!—but I could see the evidence of past storms in the few old coconut palms which lay where they had crashed. It was very still until scores of ugly frigate birds rose almost as one, angry or afraid at our intrusion, and wheeled off noisily towards the seclusion of One Tree Island.

Smithy yelled, "Let's anchor here and I'll help you into your boat. No point taking mine off the deck, Tom —not yet anyway."

Once the anchor was down, I pulled the tow-line taut, and Smithy grabbed it as I clambered aboard. The fowls looked very sorry for themselves as I cast off, then Smithy climbed in and I rowed ashore.

It was a strange moment, charged with emotion, as the boat grounded and I jumped into the warm shallow water to make her fast. In an instant the six years of waiting were wiped off the slate; it was as though they had never happened, and I felt just as if I were returning from an expedition to one of the motus and that Smithy's *Tahiti*, riding at anchor in the lagoon, was just another visiting yacht.

The beach looked just the same—a bit dirty with old palm fronds that had been blown up against the edge of the trees. But nothing had changed, as nothing had changed for a thousand years. When I stepped off the coral on to the sandy beach, I took off my rubber shoes so that I could feel the heat burning the soles of my feet.

The baleful clucking of the fowls reminded me of more mundane things. We had work to do, especially as Smithy naturally wanted to return to Raro as soon as possible for the second trip.

"But we just can't start unloading until I've had a quick look at the shack," I begged Smithy. "Who knows— it may have blown down!"

We had some difficulty forcing a way along the coral path—the path I had kept so spick and span—which was now crowded with convolvulus vine and fronds. It was just like walking through jungle, and when we reached the edge of the yard, by the corner of the shack, Smithy took one look and, scratching his head, said simply, but with complete conviction, "Tom! No one man can clean up *this* mess!"

The shack and the outhouses were completely smothered and encased by creepers, though I was glad to see that my wire guy ropes were still in position. Coconut fronds were littered all over the place. The old shed in the yard where I used to keep my tools and firewood looked even worse than the first time I had arrived on the island. One glance at the cook-house told me that I would virtually need to rebuild it; behind it, my breadfruit tree had all but disappeared under a convolvulus vine. Looking around me, I could see I would have to start all over from the beginning again. The garden was a mass of weeds and sprouting coconuts which must have fallen from the nearby palms. The garden fence and fowl run had both collapsed.

And yet I cannot remember feeling the least sensation of dismay. It was no worse than it had been in 1952, and I had managed then—at first even without a boat. Now I had better tools, larger stores and a good boat. Obviously there was going to be a long hard pull ahead to get things straight, but if I had done it once, I could do it again, and this was no time to start moaning.

"At least the shack's standing—let's have a look at that." I strode towards the veranda. The veranda was all right; my repairs following the big storm which had smashed the pier had stood up for six years, though I would have to do a bit of thatching.

As I opened the door, I started to explain to Smithy,

"This was my office." Then I stopped. The centre of the floor was a lake.

"That's where it's come from." Smithy pointed to the roof. "Nothing to worry about—we can mend that in a day."

It was a bad leak, where a section of the tin roof had been ripped off, and soon I discovered that the roof of the kai room was also leaking. However, I had hardly examined the roof before something else riveted my attention. It was a bit of paper—or rather two pieces, one white, one green—held in position on the kai bench by a lump of coral.

I picked up the white paper. It was a note dated March, 1956, and it read, "Don't know who you are or if you're returning, but would like you to know my boat stayed here two weeks. We enjoyed the fruits of your well-kept garden and ate five of your fowls. Hope this will cover everything. Sincerely, Sid P. Thatcher, San Francisco."

The other "bit of paper" was a twenty-dollar bill.

"Well, I'll be damned," said Smithy. "I didn't know there *were* any honest people left in the world."

What a pleasant gesture from the unknown Mr. Thatcher. It conjured up all sorts of thoughts. Was there a Mrs. T? Were they still alive? I kept that bill for a long, long time—until one day when it came in very handy.

"Come on, Tom!" Smithy interrupted my thoughts. "Stop thinking how you're going to spend it! I want to see more of the place."

We made our way back through the office into the bedroom. Luckily, it was as dry as a bone, without a trace of damp.

In view of the leaking roof—which wouldn't present a serious problem once I got down to it—we decided to store all my possessions in the bedroom pending my return.

First we unloaded everything on to the beach, ferrying the cases, the planks of wood, the wire netting, the fowls, from the *Tahiti* in my small boat. I lost count of the number of trips we made, but at last we had an enormous mound on the beach. While Smithy made a fire, I went fishing and came back with three large cray for lunch, after which, working almost without a break, we lugged the heavy cases up the coral path to the shack. All the cases were nailed down, though I had not been able to fasten my tins of kerosene, so for safety I now tied these up firmly between the wall and some cases.

I had to let the fowls run wild. Poor devils! When I let them out of the box, they tottered around as though drunk. It would take them quite a while to get used to dry land.

We got everything into the shack that afternoon, but by the time we had hauled my boat on to the veranda and covered it with sacking, dusk was approaching, so we decided to sleep the night on board the *Tahiti* and sail the following day.

Before we left for Raro to pick up the second load, I wrote a note on a piece of cardboard, and tacked it on the door. It said:

TO WHOM IT MAY CONCERN
PLEASE DO NOT KILL ANY OF THE ROOSTERS
OR FOWLS, OR TAKE ANY OF MY STORES OR
USE MY BOAT. I EXPECT TO RETURN IN
ABOUT THREE WEEKS.

T. NEALE

I was back on April 23.

Part Four

ON THE ISLAND

April 1960—December 1963

15. *Visitors by Helicopter*

Wₕₑₙ ɪ ᴄᴀᴍᴇ to write this book, I almost decided to end it at the point where I was taken off the island with my bad back. It seemed to me that I might become a bore by retracing old steps again in print, for after all I lived pretty much the same sort of life on my second visit as I had done on my first. I returned because I couldn't keep away from the place—my reasons for loving Suvarov have always been as uncomplicated as that—but the challenge of living again on the island, performing the same old tasks, might savour of repetition to the reader.

Then I had second thoughts, because in fact a number of fascinating incidents did break the monotony of my existence and I think you might care to read about them. Yet before I reach them I must, as briefly as I can (and at the risk of repetition) tell you how I settled down, for those first days took on a strange dream-like quality in which, though I had to fish and cook and gather my firewood, I was hardly aware of what I was doing.

I would get up in the morning, put on my pareu, brew my coffee and suddenly reflect that by rights I should be in a pair of long trousers, jangling a bunch of keys ready to open the store. I had escaped! That was the overwhelming sensation, that was what made those early days so unbelievably wonderful and precious: I had cheated authority, fate, life itself, and all by a miracle.

My second stay on Suvarov lasted over three and a half years, and during this time only six yachts called at the island; once fourteen months passed without my seeing another human being; yet I was never lonely.

The first weeks were to set a pattern of living that lasted my entire time on the island. Never again did I punish myself with long hours of physical work as I had done during my first stay. I had learned a bitter lesson then—that you cannot overwork on an island diet—and I vowed never to forget it.

Now that I had had six years to re-live every moment I had spent on the island, and to reflect on the mistakes I had made, I rather ruefully came to the conclusion that I, who loved the leisurely pace of life on the islands, had failed when I reached Suvarov the first time to put into practice the lessons learned during half a lifetime in the South Pacific. I could understand how it had happened. I had been so proud of my island that I wanted to do everything in a rush. And so, in a curiously ironic way, I had unwittingly imposed on the timeless quality of the island the speed and bustle of modern cities from which I had been so anxious to escape.

Perhaps this sounds a little exaggerated, but now that I was back I was determined not to make the same mistake again, even though I found myself faced with the same overgrown wilderness which had greeted me when I landed in 1952.

This time, however, I had better tools, better stores, and in a way a much better start. For though the garden looked an overgrown tangle of vines and weeds, at least the ravening pigs had been eliminated so that the old banana trees were flourishing and my paw-paw shoots had grown up into sizeable trees.

The fowls I had brought with me were thoroughly domesticated and this seemed to revive memories amongst

the survivors of the flock I had abandoned six years
before; so much so that almost as soon as they sighted me
they came running for food. And even surveying what
was left of their old run, I knew that now I was equipped
with my two fifty-yard rolls of wire netting, the job of
rebuilding it would be comparatively simple.

During those first weeks, I gradually tried to put the
house in order. After I had mended the roof, I painted
the inside of the kai room white, renovated the cook-
house and built a new and more permanent stove with
an oven in which I could cook dishes from the more
exciting ingredients I had brought with me. Since I
now had milk powder, I was able to make myself a baked
custard as soon as the hens started laying, and even scones
and pastry while my flour lasted.

Although it was to prove a Herculean task, I think that
remaking the garden gave me more pleasure than any
other single task, though I had my problems. Clearing
away the jumble of vines was only the beginning. I
discovered that the topsoil which remained underneath
was choked with weeds, so that at first it seemed that, no
matter how many I wrenched up, others would have
sprung up in their place the following day. Once I had
cleared a space I would rake over a bed for my seedlings
until not a living thing showed above the carefully prepared soil. But it seemed I had only to turn my back or a
couple of heavy showers to come down before the place
would be alive again with joyful green sprouts. If only
seeds would grow as fast as weeds! When, finally, the
seeds did start to thrust through the poor soil, I was often
unable to decide which were weeds and which were seeds,
so that I was forced to let the weeds grow unmolested
until I was eventually able to tell the difference. And
then, just as they really started to look promising, as
like as not in would come my old friends (or their

descendants) the tiny hermit crabs, and nip off all the tender shoots. It was almost as though they had been waiting patiently for me to weed the garden to make life easier for them.

Beyond the garden the jungle had to be cleared too, for the path to the beach was now so overgrown in places that I had to saw away heavy limbs which had burgeoned from the trees during my absence. Over the past six years the winds had piled up enormous heaps of dead branches and fronds, almost—as though out of spite— exactly where I needed plenty of freedom to move about.

I was constantly busy with machete or axe. Much of the debris I cleared came in useful as firewood, and I always had my eye open for handy saplings or sticks to tie up my tomato plants which, now that they had room to breathe, were growing with amazing rapidity.

Imperceptibly, without any apparent period of transition, I slipped gently back into the well-remembered routine—at a slower tempo, however, which meant that though I still had plenty to keep me occupied, I felt no guilt when I took a day off. Now that I had a really sturdy boat, this temptation was much greater.

I began to make periodic excursions to all the tiny islets in the lagoon, and on one good day, with the wind in the right quarter, I actually covered the six miles to Motu Tuo, in two hours. Once there, the weather seemed so perfect that on an impulse I decided to remain on the islet for the night.

Though I am quite used to sleeping outside, a sudden thought now struck me. Robinson Crusoe had built himself a secondary residence some miles away from his stockade. Why shouldn't I do the same? What was to stop me having a "summer house" on Motu Tuo, so that, if I ever felt bored, I could sail or row over for a change of scenery?

I was seized with enthusiasm and spent all day building a rough lean-to out of coconut fronds. Then I speared some ku, picked some wild paw-paw and cooked supper of grilled fish and baked fruit on the beach in front of my new house, washing it down with coconut water in place of my usual cup of tea.

Only one minor incident ruined this idyllic expedition. I woke with a yell in the middle of the night as a sudden pain transfixed my leg so violently that it felt as though my calf had been slashed open with a knife. There was no moon, and I was without a lamp, but as instinctively I bent down to touch my leg I felt the sticky wetness of blood in the darkness and became aware of something moving and shuffling close beside my hand.

I had forgotten those damned coconut crabs! The cruel nip didn't appear to have done any serious damage, but I got no more sleep that night after washing my wound in salt water, And on my next trip to Motu Tuo, in self preservation, I took a saw, hammer and nails and made myself a bunk, from odd bits of driftwood.

Over the months (though I worked only when I felt so inclined) my shack on Motu Tuo became quite comfortable. It never had the permanence of my home on Anchorage, but I rigged up some shelves for crockery and pots and pans which I left there, together with a spare hurricane lamp, some kerosene and two boxes of matches, each sealed in separate water-tight tins—a precaution I took in case I got doused when sailing over. On one occasion I stayed there a week, taking with me some more tools, and built a more permanent bed, and then re-thatched the roof and walls with pandanus which, if well done, will outlast coconut thatching by many years. I laid in a big stock of firewood and built a rough but serviceable cook-house just behind the shack. The only drawback was the complete lack of water which I needed for my evening cup of tea on the beach. The trouble was, I had nothing to serve as a receptacle in which I could store the rain, and though I toyed with the idea of scouring out an old oil drum and taking it over, I discarded the plan because I didn't relish the thought of drinking water which might have been uncovered for a month between my visits. In the end I compromised and carried bottles of water over each time I made the trip.

I loved my little excursions to Moto Tuo, for though it was not as beautiful as "my" island, it was surprising how pleasant a change of scenery could be.

Moto Tuo, where Frisbie had once jokingly suggested I should live, was almost as large as Anchorage, but the other islets like One Tree (where my back had seized up) and Brushwood were so small that I seldom visited them except for my brief trips in search of valuable flotsam.

And so time seemed almost to float on from week to week so effortlessly that had I not faithfully entered up my journal every evening, I could hardly have believed six months had already passed.

They were months which had seen great changes. The garden was now flourishing, I had pollinated the blossoms, re-thatched the veranda roof and repainted the inside of the shack. The fowl population had multiplied, the coconut crabs had been killed off. But during all that time I had never once seen a sail on the horizon, nor an aircraft overhead. I had been utterly alone, and utterly content.

Without warning in November 1960 the silence which enveloped the island—broken only by the boom of the surf and the crying of birds—was suddenly shattered by a roar which made the old cat run for her life and sent the hens fluttering into the illusionary security of their coop. It was so unexpected that for one moment I too froze with fear, and I remember it flashed through my mind that another war must have started.

I ran out of the shack in a panic as the roaring became louder and more ominous. From the cover of the coconut trees I looked up and saw two enormous shadows in the sky, as monstrous and as predatory as the frigate birds now flying away in protest. Then I realised—they were two helicopters.

Until they hovered almost directly over the shack I thought perhaps they were going to leave me alone. I was still hidden in the trees, but now I ran down the coral path and waited in the shelter of the palms edging the beach by the old pier as the leading helicopter slowly came down in front of me with a flurry of wings which blew dust everywhere. When she finally settled—even more like a bird than before—the giant blades stopped rotating, a door was thrust open and two men in khaki drill stepped out. Almost immediately afterwards, the second helicopter landed a few yards farther along the beach. From their behaviour it was quite obvious to me that none of the men had the slightest suspicion there was anyone on this tiny island, and I hope I may be forgiven for introducing a touch of drama. As they stood there, one of them pushing back his peaked cap to wipe the sweat off his forehead, I stepped out of the trees, raised my battered old hat and said, "United States Navy, I presume?"

I have never seen two men so stunned with surprise. Both stood there gaping for fully ten seconds until one of them, recovering his wits, stepped back a pace, saluted smartly, then walked forward and shook hands. It was a signal to end the "formalities."

"Well, I'll be damned!" he gasped. "What in hell's name are you doing here?"

"I live here!" I replied.

"Alone?"

"Yes, alone—you're the first person I've spoken to for six months."

They were all crowding around me, and one offered me a cigarette, looked at my skin the colour of mahogany and said rather doubtfully, "You don't look like a native, sir."

"I'm not," I replied simply, "I'm a New Zealander."

"Well, by God!" he cried. "It's lucky for you we've called. Now we can get you off."

As yet they had no conception I was on the island because I *wanted* to be. One of them told me eagerly that their ship—which I could now see outside the lagoon—was going to New Zealand, and he was quite sure they could "rescue" me and give me a lift back to civilisation.

"But I *like* it here!" I replied, almost unable to stop chuckling.

The senior officer scratched his brown hair again, and muttered, "Well, I'll be darned! Robinson Crusoe come true."

I took them on a tour of my shack, and discovered they belonged to an American icebreaker, the *Glacier*, on its way to the Antarctic via New Zealand. She was still steaming ahead, so they could not stay, otherwise she would move outside flying range and they might become marooned with me!

They had flown over "for a practice spin" and with the idea of collecting a few drinking nuts. I split some for them as they examined every detail of the shack, the garden, the fowl run, still finding it difficult to believe that such a state of affairs could exist in the twentieth century.

"Are you *sure* you don't want to string along with us?" one asked.

Very shortly they were ready to go. Our farewells were marked by much handshaking and delving into pockets which yielded up all the half-empty packets of cigarettes they happened to have with them.

"Gee," said one ruefully, "we could have brought you anything you wanted if we'd only known you were here."

We talked a minute or so longer and they promised to contact my sister in New Zealand to let her know I was in good health. Then one said, almost awkwardly, "Sorry, Mr. Neale, we just gotta go. Orders are orders and half an hour was the limit. But it's been wonderful meeting you."

They climbed aboard, waved farewell, and with a flurry of rotors and a cloud of dust, rose up back into the air bound for the twentieth century again.

When I returned to the shack, the old cat had crept back and the fowls were already busy pecking in the run.

Their entire visit had occupied half an hour—the briefest visit anybody has ever yet paid to Suvarov.

The landing of the helicopters was to have an interesting sequel. Though I knew nothing of it at the time, the U.S. Navy released a brief news item about their visit to Suvarov, and this was how Noel Barber, the author and journalist, first heard about me whilst recovering in hospital from a car crash. Apparently he decided he wanted to see the island—and me—and arrived about five months later in the *Manua Tele*, which he had chartered in Pago Pago.

When he landed Noel was still only able to walk with the aid of sticks for he had been badly smashed up, but he stayed two days, and brought me a liberal supply of stores which included tea, flour, corned beef, together with whisky, rum and cigarettes. He also brought with him Chuck Smouse, an American photographer, and he and Noel took many of the photographs which appear in this book.

I was so touched by the stores they had brought for me that when the *Manua Tele* had sailed, I sat down in the office and wrote Noel Barber a long letter of thanks. It was fourteen months before that letter left the island; for it was fourteen months before the next ship called in at Suvarov. Call in it did eventually, however, and under the most unexpected circumstances.

One morning I had just washed my face and was about to sip my breakfast coffee when suddenly I heard a ship's whistle—a particular whistle I knew as well as my own voice.

"Well, I'll be damned!" I cried out loud. "The *Tiare Taporo*. It must be Andy!"

Leaving my coffee untasted, I ran down to the beach—and there was the *Tiare Taporo*, lying in the passage. Two Cook Islanders were already half-way to the pier in the ship's boat.

The moment I saw the *Tiare* lying in the passage I knew she wouldn't be staying long. Andy knew the lagoon so well that, had he intended to remain, he would have sailed right in and anchored.

As the ship's boat beached, I recognised one of the boys amongst the crew who cried "Hallo Tom!" Once they were on the shore I saw they had a native passenger who greeted me by shaking hands solemnly but eyeing me, I thought, a trifle queerly—almost as though I were an apparition.

"Is Andy still captain?" I inquired.

I was assured that he was—and he was anxious to see me. They were ready to row me to the *Tiare* right away.

Begging them to wait a few moments, I nipped back to

the shack and took out Mr. Thatcher's twenty-dollar bill from the tin box where I kept my "petty cash" (to pay yachtsmen who kindly posted my letters) together with some mail for Andy to post.

Then we set off for the *Tiare* and before long I could see Andy standing on the poop. I boarded her at the stern, climbing up by the after rigging, then made my way to the poop where Andy came forward to meet me with his usual hearty handshake.

I think this moment of meeting was the first time I can remember feeling a little lonely. In the ordinary way meeting visitors never moved me deeply, but Andy was my oldest friend, he was a direct link with my past, with Raro, with half my life. To see him standing there brought a lump to my throat and took me right back to the big veranda several miles out of Raro where we had so often spent an evening.

But the instant of emotion vanished the moment he spoke.

"Tom!" he cried. "Thank God you're alive!"

I looked at him in astonishment. "Is there any reason why I shouldn't be?" I asked.

"Don't you know?" he replied slowly. "Haven't they—" with a jerk of the head to the boat's crew— "told you? You're supposed to be dead!"

I burst out laughing.

"Come into the cabin and have a drink—" Andy's voice was almost brusque—"and I'll tell you all about it."

Down in the main cabin I remembered so well that it was almost like home, opposite this man who had been my friend for over thirty years, I gratefully sipped my first drink for over a year and listened to the most astounding story.

He had been sailing from Puka Puka back home to Rarotonga, Andy explained, when he received a radio message from the Resident Commissioner—a new one, for Mr. Nevill had long since gone. The message was brief and to the point. A strong rumour had reached Rarotonga that a Japanese fishing boat calling in at Suvarov had found my body.

Looking at me over his drink, Andy said soberly, "The *Tiare Taporo* was ordered to call in, investigate and if necessary give you a Christian burial."

"A Japanese fisherman!" I burst out laughing again. "But Andy—you're the first man I've seen for fourteen months."

"Well, I'm more than delighted to see it was only a rumour," said Andy dryly.

"But how could a rumour like that start?"

"Your guess is as good as mine," Andy confessed. "I got the radio message, that's all. Let's forget it— come on, Tom, have another drink."

Time means money to a ship, and Andy was not the owner of the *Tiare Taporo*, so his visit was brief—though not quite so brief as that of the Americans in their helicopters, for he stayed in the passage for over two hours whilst we gossiped about friends in Rarotonga and what was happening in the outside world.

There was so much to talk about, however unimportant, that the time seemed to fly, and I found myself hoping until the very last minute that he would stay a little longer. After all, it was Andy who had taken me to the island in the first place.

But though we had another drink and yarned for a little while longer, Andy finally said reluctantly, "I'll have to be on my way. Sorry I can't stay longer, Tom, and come ashore—do you remember that first picnic on Motu Tuo?—but I'm under orders."

Before leaving, I bought a tin of cabin bread and some tobacco from the ship's store, and Andy gave me a bottle of rum. As I was getting ready to say good-bye and step down into the boat alongside, I could not resist saying, "Don't forget to let them know that I'm alive."

"I've already radioed—the news'll be round Raro tonight that you're fit and well." He paused, shifted from one foot to the other and then said seriously, "Make sure you stay that way, Tom."

My parting words as I climbed down his after rigging were, "You'll have to wait a long time yet before you bury me!"

I stood on the old pier until the *Tiare* had faded from sight, feeling rather sad, wondering what they were doing on board, reflecting that in a few days Andy would be back in the "civilisation" I so despised, yet which now, suddenly and for the first time, seemed to have its desirable qualities. Almost despondently I could picture Andy returning to his bungalow, I could visualise his garden with its African daisies, then I had a sudden picture in my mind's eye of the stores on Main Street. As I stood gazing out past the lagoon to the open sea, I thought that I wouldn't have minded returning to Raro for a fortnight's holiday.

The old cat, rubbing against my bare ankle, brought me back to reality.

"Don't be a sentimental old fool, Neale," I said severely. "You know damned well you'd hate it after a week."

All the same, when I reached the shack I poured out half a tumbler of Andy's excellent rum. It was the only time I ever took a drink alone during the daytime. But then, that was the only time I really needed it.

16. Five Hours in the Water

I HAVE NEVER in my life encountered any natural force more relentless than the Pacific Ocean. Sometimes it almost put me in mind of an enemy biding its time, awaiting the one moment when I might be off my guard.

Consequently, I never took a chance and never took my boat out should the barometer show the slightest sign of impending bad weather, because I knew only too well how swiftly the Pacific can change her moods; one moment calm and tranquil, the next a cauldron of titanic force. Nor did I ever let a week go by without examining my box of tools, which would be my only insurance against survival should a hurricane sweep over the island.

And yet—through no fault of my own—I suddenly found myself one morning, in July 1961, struggling for my life when my boat capsized in the middle of the lagoon.

I didn't know it then, but I was to be in the water for five hours.

There had been no warning. We had been experiencing a short spell of bad weather, but this was over now and we were well out of reach of the hurricane season. The barometer stood high, and that morning, which dawned as placidly as any I can remember, there seemed nothing on earth to prevent me sailing the five miles to Bird Island on one of my "tours of inspection" to see if anything of value had been washed up on the beach.

Five Hours in the Water

I reached the motu aided by a good breeze, collected one or two useful bits of flotsam and by midday I was on my way back to Anchorage. I was in the middle of the lagoon, in about a hundred and fifty feet of water, when a squall rose right out of nowhere and hit us. Within a few seconds everything had changed. The sun had vanished, the clouds grew horridly black and the wind started screaming. Plainly we were in for a sudden sharp squall—the sort which could be on one in a few minutes. I did not even have time to lower the sail, but simply rapidly pushed up the boom and sail, making sure the main sheet was free to run. Next I lashed it to the mast, a trick I had long ago learned for getting sail off quickly. Altogether the whole job took less than a minute, so that I had the boat trimmed before the squall had a chance to reach its height. I still had the jib set. I would be able to sail it out, and was quite confident. Obviously the next hour or so looked like being thoroughly rough and uncomfortable, but perfectly safe so long as I resigned myself to being tossed about like a cork.

But as the storm gathered force—and I could see it sweeping towards me across the lagoon—I began to have doubts.

It was astonishing how rapidly the sea rose with the force of the wind. Suddenly shivering a little, I remembered a description in one of Frisbie's books of how heavy seas tearing through the pass would meet a comber inside the lagoon and explode in a cloud of spray.

This was exactly what *did* happen. Within a few minutes the coral ring had become a cloud of spume and the waves inside the lagoon started gathering ever-increasing force and size. Over above Brushwood and Turtle—the nearest motus—I could see clouds of black frigate birds being blown all over the place despite their four-foot wing span. The great waves hitting each other far out across the reef were forming gushers which curtained off every speck of land.

I was still not really worried, for the force of the heavy seas roaring through the pass was still well south of me, so that the combers came rolling in from east to west. In actual fact I was only getting the backwash, so that, though drenched, I was able to stand the buffeting well until unexpectedly a stronger gust overtook us. What happened next ought, by rights, never to have occurred. I had stowed the sail carefully away when I tied the boom to the mast, but this freak gust seemed to bite into it and sneak inside so that before I could move, the sail was bellying out above the mast.

I knew immediately that I must act swiftly since otherwise I would be in real danger of capsizing. Cautiously, but as rapidly as I dared, I clambered on to the forward thwart, where I stood, hugging the mast with one arm, and trying to secure the wildly flapping sail.

I almost succeeded when another gust caught us and the sail bellied out right into my face. Without warning, the boat gently keeled over. I couldn't do a thing. One moment I was standing there helpless, waiting, as my twelve-footer sl wly turned right over beneath me—so slowly that the next minute I almost stepped into the water.

A wave caught me, forcing me under the warm water. When I surfaced, eyes smarting with the salt, gasping, spitting out sea water, I found I had been swept several yards away from the boat. Everything was so confused —the big waves were charging at me all the time—that at first I thought I'd lost the boat, for it was all so dark— the darkness of storm clouds covering the sky. Then I saw a patch of white and knew the boat at least was safe —even if upside down. I struck out towards her, and tried to grab her for support but it was impossible to obtain any hold on that smooth bottom.

Luckily I was thoroughly at home in the water, a legacy of my old Tahiti days. I knew that somewhere under the water the mast must be pointing downwards, and felt confident that if I could only get a grip on it, give it a sharp jerk and a heave, I might have a chance of turning her upright again. It was not so much a question of strength; given a well-placed shove, a capsized boat with a mast will naturally tend to move upwards in the right direction.

I took a deep breath and submerged. But I had under-estimated my task. Time after time I had to dive before I was able to grab the mast by its tip. I knew that once I caught hold of it I would have to swim under water and push it with one hand whilst I kicked out with my feet. Fortunately the water at midday was warm, but I think I must have had to dive ten or a dozen times. The struggle seemed never-ending. Each time I shot to the surface for air, I ha no support on which to rest and was forced to dog-paddle whilst getting a breather. Finally I managed to reach the mast and give it one enormous jerk. Immediately it seemed to give, to slip away from my pushing fingers.

I followed it up until I could feel the wind on my face, and as I gulped in air and spray and trod water in the violent chop, I felt something brush my leg. I knew at once that if it were a shark there was nothing I could do. But the solid feel of it told me that this was no shark. It was the mast.

It was horizontal at last, just under the waves, and I grabbed it and had my first real rest, leaning across it, indifferent as wave after wave swept over me, just hanging on grimly, half submerged, wondering what on earth I was going to do next. For a moment I toyed with the idea of trying to push the mast out of the water. But I abandoned this plan since I knew that were I to let go of it for long the waves would sweep me away.

However, now the mast was level on the water, it was acting in the same way as a spar on an outrigger canoe, and now the boat was on her side I had at least a sort of floating platform to support me. If I wanted to right her, however, there was only one thing to do— get the mast out. And this was impossible until the wind went down. Hanging on there, I tried to open my eyes between the waves that kept coming over me. I wanted to see the sky, the clouds. It seemed—from the brief glimpses I could manage—that the sky was growing lighter. I knew from experience that these storms are violent but short-lived. And so I prepared to "sit it out" hanging on to the mast, waiting until the waves were smaller, more infrequent, so I could tread water without fear of drifting away from the boat.

The squall must have lasted an hour or more, and curiously enough—or perhaps, on reflection, it was natural—I do not remember ever being afraid of sharks during all that time. I never saw one, and I suppose I was too busy holding on to my boat—and my life—to think about them. I suppose in fact that all this time I must have been acting instinctively.

The wait seemed interminable—so long that when finally I found myself waiting for the next wave to fill my eyes with stinging salt water and it didn't come, I could hardly believe my good fortune. Raising myself slightly in the water I looked around. It was still choppy, but the sea was definitely beginning to quieten. Waves still hit me from time to time, but failed to push me under. The sky, too, had lightened from black to grey, and as I floated, one hand clutching the mast, I noticed a sliver

of blue in the sky—and knew the sun must be trying
to struggle through. All at once life seemed much more
cheerful!

Fortified with the new energy this realisation seemed
to summon up, I now set about the major task of getting
the mast and sails off the boat. It took at least an hour.
I remember later, when I told somebody how I had
managed this job, he told me flatly that it was impossible,
but in fact, given strength and patience, it wasn't so
difficult as one might imagine.

But it certainly seemed to take an age. First I had to
free the rigging—the two back stays and the fore stay.
These were made of wire, but were fastened down with
rope lashings which had swollen and were difficult to
free when I dived under for short bursts. However, I
managed to undo them. Next I had to dive to free the
jib sheets—a simpler job because they were only fastened
to the cleats. I had to take several rests, clinging with
one hand to the mast to support myself and give my legs a
rest.

My next job was to haul all this gear I had dis-
mantled into a sort of state where I could wrap it round
the boom and then try to lash the whole unwieldy lot
roughly to the mast, which was still lying a little under the
water. I managed this by wrapping the loose ends of the
ropes round everything until I had boom, sails and all
attached in a rough bundle to the mast.

Now I surveyed the mast itself which had been stepped
by being passed down through a half loop of brass
fastened to a timber which in turn was made fast to each
gunwale. It was a simple design, so that the foot of the
mast fitted into a notch in another piece of timber fastened
to the keelson. I had deliberately designed it this way
so that, though it was strong, I could easily step the mast
unaided by merely lifting it up, dropping it through the

half-loop and into the notch. It was not, of course, permanently fastened.

Getting it out, however, proved much more difficult than I had anticipated. Since the boat was lying on her side, the weight of the mast—encumbered by its bulky burden of sail and boom—made the butt jam in the loop.

I couldn't budge it at first and though the wind had fallen a lot by now, and the chop was not too bad, I had been in the water for some hours and was beginning to tire.

Each fresh attempt seemed more wearying. Every time I held on to the boat with one hand and tried to free the mast with the other, I found I was too clos to get a proper leverage. Finally I decided I would have to use both hands, so after clinging to the boat to regain a little strength, I swam to where the tip of the mast lay just under the waves, and grabbed hold of it, kicking as hard as I could with my feet, and violently jerking and pulling it up and down to get it free. To my delight my efforts were almost immediately rewarded. At the first attempt I could feel it had left its step at the bottom of the boat.

But in its wake this victory seemed to conjure up a new hazard. For almost at the moment I felt the mast loosen, it started to swing. I clutched at it, endeavouring to keep it steady, for I knew that were the loop of soft brass to bend under this pressure, the mast would jam irretrievably. If I were ever to get it free, it was now no longer a question of brute force. What was needed was a gentle, coaxing pull and a pretty constantly maintained pressure in order to keep the mast as straight as possible while I slowly tugged it free through the loop.

Treading water all the time, I used one hand to balance and swim and held on to the mast with the other, kicking as I carefully manoeuvred it inch by inch through the loop.

And at last I managed it, too exhausted now to experience anything but a profound feeling of relief. I didn't have to worry about it floating away; it lay, with all the sails attached, a soggy mass in the water.

After that it was fairly simple to right the boat. I swam round, climbed over the opposite side and put my foot on the centreboard. She righted herself immediately and I let go and fell back into the waves before my weight sank her, for amidships she was barely an inch or two above water.

I had lost my baler when she capsized, so after hanging on to the gunwale until I regained my breath, I tried to start scooping some of the   ater out of her with my hands. The wind had eased up considerably by now but the seas were still rough enough to slop into the boat, until, holding on with both hands and kicking with my feet, I managed to turn her bows into the wind. Gripping one gunwale with my right hand, I began splashing out water with my left. For over an hour I was forced to keep on baling madly with intervals for rests. Every so often she would swing broadside to the waves and the water would start to slop in again so that it seemed as though I would never make any real headway. Amidships she was still barely two inches above the water, but I kept on doggedly in the knowledge that the wind was continuing to drop.

Nearly an hour later—it may have been longer but I had lost count of time—I suddenly began to realise that she was imperceptibly rising in the water. And the sun was breaking through! From then on I took great care to keep her head on to the seas and frequently had to swim away from my task to slew her round. Even today, so long afterwards, I still only remember one particular moment during this long-drawn struggle, as I hung on to the gunwale, getting my breath back, crying out loud, "Neale! You're not going to let this beat you."

And I didn't because, simply through sticking at it, I kept on baling until eventually I had three inches of freeboard at the lowest part of the sheer. By now I was so tired that this seemed like the promised land and I decided I would try and get into the boat. I knew it would be fatal to try and clamber in over the side so, having made sure her bows were well into the seas, I summoned up what strength I had left and swam round to the bows where I climbed quickly and carefully inboard. To my relief, I found she was just able to bear my weight without going down. But it was a near thing and I didn't dare to rest, not even for a second. I sat down on the midship thwart and baled like mad with cupped hands. It is amazing what a lot of water you can shift this way; before long I had four inches of freeboard and only then did I take a brief rest.

Now at last I felt safe and all I had to do was go on ladling out water until it was low enough for me to haul in the bundle of mast, sail and boom, and make for home.

I did not have the strength to try and set the mast to sail home, but fortunately the oars had been well stowed and had remained in the boat all the time. I dragged them out and wearily started rowing for Anchorage.

I reached Anchorage at dusk, and not until I was rubbing myself down in the shack did I notice that all the skin on the inside of my left arm had been rubbed off. Each time I had scooped out the water, I must have rasped my arm against the gunwale.

I was too tired to bother about it, for as I wrote in my journal that evening, "There's no need for a rocking chair tonight."

17. The Castaways

No VESSEL CAME in to Suvarov for many months after Andy had left, but by now I was too occupied and happy to take much notice of lack of human contact. Everything was going splendidly. I was getting three crops of tomatoes a year, plenty of melons, cucumbers, onions and sweet potatoes; more breadfruit and bananas than I could eat, and though I had long since used up my flour, my patch of cassava made an excellent substitute for puddings. I had a fair amount of tea (given to me by Noel Barber) but I hoarded it carefully, using the leaves over and over again. Nor was I short of eggs or a rooster for the pot since by now there were fifty fowls in the hen house. Even the fact that I had run out of tobacco did not worry me. I just seemed to be immune to the craving which had tortured me when this had happened before, a happy state of affairs which confirmed what I had always suspected: that my desire for tobacco (and meat) had been brought about by overwork during the time I was building the pier.

I could have found some substitute for the tobacco had I wished, for many Cook Islanders smoke banana leaves rolled up tightly to form a sort of local cigar, though believe me it has a vastly different flavour. I had tried them before now and discovered they were not unpleasant, but fortunately I had reached the stage where for the moment anyway I did not need tobacco. I would have thoroughly enjoyed a cigarette had someone offered me one, but I couldn't be bothered to roll my own banana cigars.

Though time was really of no consequence, some inhibition from the past, some subconscious need to maintain some link with the outside world, impelled me to keep careful track of the days, months and years. I had no calendar, so I made my own as I went along, using small pieces of paper which I divided into thirty squares. Each day after I had collected and counted the eggs I wrote the number down in a square, adding a day and date to the previous square—taking care at the end of each month to remember that invaluable schoolboy rhyme "Thirty days hath September" and putting two sets of figures in one square when necessary.

Since I had to collect eggs, I rather enjoyed keeping the record straight, and entering the date alongside the number of eggs became a formality to which I meticulously adhered. As a double check I used to copy the date from my home-made calendar into the exercise books which served as my journal. I wrote these up every evening—always starting with the barometer reading and following with the day's events, though I doubt if any were as staggering as the entry for August 30, 1963 when I wrote, "Got the biggest shock of my life today. Was sitting on the veranda plaiting some fronds for a hole in the veranda roof, when some instinct caused me to look up. Standing there, silently observing me, was a tall, thin man, dressed in a pareu and Hawaiian-style flowered shirt. My heart seemed to stop beating for a second at the sight until my fear gave way to anger."

I remember my first words, blurted out in a fury of shock and surprise were, "What the hell do you mean—"

The Castaways

It was only as he began to stammer a reply that I realised he was almost more flabbergasted than I.

"I'd no idea—" he began. "I thought this island was uninhabited."

"Who are you?" I asked a little more civilly.

He told me his name was Ed Vessey and explained he was an American travelling in his yacht with his Samoan wife and daughter from Pago-Pago to Honolulu. They had put into the lagoon for a spell of rest after a windless passage during which it had taken them twelve days to travel four hundred miles.

"I'm real sorry if I scared you," he added, "but, honestly, I was a damn' sight more frightened than you. When I saw you I tried to holler, but the words just wouldn't come out."

"That's all right," I said more cheerfully, for I was in fact delighted to see a new face. "Let's go down to your boat."

"Okay," he agreed, adding tactfully after one look at my loincloth, "Maybe you'd care to put a few more clothes on. There's a couple of ladies down on the beach."

I hurried inside the shack and for the first time in nearly a year donned a pair of shorts.

Dressed in my respectable attire I was delighted to meet Ed Vessey's wife, a jolly, chain-smoking Samoan, and their daughter, Sileia, a delightful child of thirteen or fourteen. Behind them in the lagoon lay their beautiful yacht.

"She's called the *Tiburon*," said Vessey. "She's a forty-footer, sleeps six and has a good auxiliary engine."

"She's a real beauty," I exclaimed, not without a trace of envy.

Three nights later she was a wreck and I had three castaways on my hands.

It happened without warning. The day had been fine and I had spent the afternoon on the *Tiburon* with the family, Mrs. Vessey entertaining us with songs which she played on her guitar. We had a drink or two and then I rowed ashore.

Just before I turned in, I happened to look out of the veranda. Some tea-towels hanging out to dry were swaying and flapping in a breeze, but I did not give the matter a second thought. Sudden short and vicious squalls were nothing new on Suvarov, and the *Tiburon* was anchored well inside the lagoon.

I settled down, read a chapter of Conrad, turned out the lamp and was fast asleep when a cry of "Tom!" woke me instantly. I scrambled out of bed, for I recognised Ed's voice, which sounded as though it must have come from the veranda. I remember wondering almost irritably, "What the devil is Ed doing here at this time of night?"

Then out of the darkness his voice came clear again above the wind, a statement so curiously worded that I have never forgotten it.

"Tom!" There was anguish, not fear in his voice. "No more *Tiburon*!"

I couldn't believe it. This was no real storm, it hadn't even started to hum through my guy ropes. I could find nothing to reply but, "What?" while I lit my hurricane lamp. As I walked out to the veranda Ed cried again, "No more *Tiburon*!"

And there on the veranda stood Ed, his wife and their daughter. I held up the lamp to see them better, for dark, swiftly scudding clouds had hidden the moon. They were standing huddled together, dripping wet, their life-jackets still around their necks.

"For God's sake come in!" I said and hustled them into my bedroom where I collected some blankets.

"Here, wrap these round you. Don't bother right now telling me what's happened. Let me get you some tea."

I piled a few chips on my smouldering tauhunu and soon had a kettle going. Only after they had taken off their wet clothes and had had a hot drink did I ask what had happened.

"We'd just turned in," Ed said flatly, "It was blowing like hell, but I wasn't worried—then without warning the cable parted. I felt the *Tiburon* move—she seemed to slew round—I was out of my bunk like a flash. I didn't even have time to get my false teeth. I'd taken them out because they were hurting. As soon as I got on deck I shouted to the others to get up while I started the motor. Sileia and her mother came up at once and started to free the dinghy—just in case. But I still wasn't *that* scared."

He sipped some more tea, and I can remember that scene in my bedroom as vividly as though it had happened yesterday. There they were—all three of them wrapped in blankets, reminding me in the dim light of my hurricane lamp of pictures I had seen as a child of a huddled group of Red Indians engaged in some momentous pow-wow.

"You haven't got a cigarette?" wailed Mrs. Vessey. I shook my head.

As Ed went on with his story, I gathered that he had tried to swing the *Tiburon* round with the idea of getting farther into the lagoon, but evidently the length of cable hanging from her bows made her sluggish in answering the helm. Nor was there any light on the island to give him some sense of direction.

"Before I could do a thing," he said miserably, "she went straight into a coral head. It must have ripped a hell of a hole up near the bows—I think it was on the starboard side, but it was all over so quickly, I couldn't take everything in. Tom—" he was almost in tears—"she

sank in a matter of minutes. The girls just had time to
free the dinghy. We jumped in as she actually went
under. We didn't have a second to grab anything—
except *that*." He jerked his head towards his wife's
guitar which she must have picked up at the last moment.
It was the one and only thing they had brought with
them.

After sighting the island in a brief moment of moonlight, they had managed to row ashore. Landing near
the north tip, they had stumbled along the beach and
the shallows until they came to the pier.

From that night the four of us shared my bedroom.
From that night onward my entire life was transformed.
No longer was I the solitary inhabitant of an island
occasionally unbending to welcome guests. I had
become one of four people—three of whom I hardly knew.
Moreover, my castaways might well have to endure their
exile in my company for months, even years. They
possessed virtually no clothes, no provisions—in fact
nothing but a guitar and the garments in which they
stood. And though by now I was accustomed, even
delighted, to welcome the occasional stranger from a
visiting yacht, I had inevitably become so set in my
ways that the very prospect of sharing my life with these
benighted strangers appalled me. There and then I
made a vow that however long they stayed I would let
no woman into my kitchen! I was so proud of my
culinary arrangements, my new stove, my painfully
acquired mastery over fires, that the idea of any woman
setting foot in my preserves filled me with a sense of
horror.

So the next morning I was careful to nip into the
kitchen quickly where I cooked breakfasts of coffee and
eggs for the lot of us. After that Ed and I went to take
a look at the wreck. We found her resting on the bottom

alongside the coral head, with her bows submerged under the high tide, so that only the forepart of her cabin top and her mast were visible above water. Since she was resting at an angle, jammed against the coral head, I said to Ed, "I think we'd better wait for the ebbing tide. Then we might be able to climb aboard."

Within an hour or so we were back on the *Tiburon*. As the tide fell, her bows stuck out of the water and only the stern remained submerged. She was awash fore and aft of course, even at low tide, so the hull was obviously filled with water, but now we were able to clamber over the bows and wade across the decks.

All at once an exciting new prospect opened up before us.

"Why can't we salvage her?" I asked Ed. "You're a castaway—just like Robinson Crusoe—remember how much stuff *he* got off the wreck."

"But the cabin, Tom?" Ed seemed dubious. "How could either of us hold our breath long enough to pick up anything worthwhile when we dive in there?"

"It's not holding my breath that worries me," I said, thinking of my diving days in Tahiti and how only a short time ago I had dived time and again to save my boat when she had capsized. "It's what happens when you get there. It's easy enough to keep your eyes open when you're swimming underwater but it's going to be more difficult groping about for small things in a water-filled cabin. How do we find your teeth for instance?"

"What I wouldn't give to get them back!" sighed Ed and then added, "I'll tell you what I *do* have—a mask. It's not a snorkel—you can't breathe with it—but it's got a big watertight glass that covers your face."

This was exactly what I needed.

Ed swore he knew just where it was in the main cabin, so the next day at low tide found us climbing aboard again. Since the mask was all-important, we had decided that Ed should make the first "dive"—or rather "venture"—into the submerged cabin, since he knew exactly where it was located. After that we would each dive in turn.

We sloshed our way through the water on the deck until we reached the top of the companionway leading down to the main saloon, where Ed and his wife had been sleeping just before she sank.

Getting in did not prove half as difficult as we had imagined. Ed climbed gingerly down the companionway, his head still above water until he had reached the bottom rung. Then he took a deep breath and went under whilst I waited, standing with the water around my knees. Although he could hardly have been down there for more than a minute, it seemed an age until Ed reappeared gasping below me on the steps. Standing on the bottom rung, his head just above water, he drew a deep breath and triumphantly held the mask aloft. He had found it at first go.

This was the beginning of a fortnight of diving for "hidden treasure"—which included everything from toothpaste to binoculars.

We soon formed a fairly regular schedule. I would start the day with breakfast, then the ladies would wash up, clean the shack and gather firewood while Ed and I went down to the yacht at low tide. Ed was still desperate to regain his teeth, but his wife seemed heartlessly obsessed with the need for us to dredge up some cartons of cigarettes. She explained their exact location to me in the minutest detail.

"I put them in a locker just above my bunk," she kept insisting until I found it difficult to refrain from retorting, "And a fat lot of good *they're* going to be after a week in salt water."

Poor girl—she really was a compulsive smoker. As soon as we had set off on our diving expeditions, she would leave Sileia—who was a quiet unobtrusive girl, not exactly pretty but very pleasant and kind—and hasten off into the bush to collect young banana leaves. These she rolled with expert speed and dexterity. She was seldom without one in her mouth.

Although Ed and I made between thirty and forty dives a day, each lasting a minute or so, her cartons of cigarettes still remained unsalvaged. Indeed there was no question of our being able to look for specific objects. All we could do was to go under and grab whatever was nearest.

It was an eerie sensation down in the cabin. Though the place was completely filled with water the *Tiburon* was only just below the water line and light came streaming in through the portholes, so that I was able to see quite clearly through my mask. I experienced a feeling of levitation, for the water through which I waded, holding my breath, was filled with strange objects that seemed to defy gravity—torn books, papers, charts, odds and ends of clothing all floated about me weightlessly as I flailed around.

Unfortunately, after a week or so these papers and books began to disintegrate, so that diving became more difficult, for one had to move through water so thick with minute particles of paper that it was almost impossible to see.

Amongst the first things we salvaged were the Vesseys' clothes and bedding. Between us we heaved out all their clothes, three mattresses, their blankets, sheets and even towels. These we loaded into my boat, and soon had them laid out on the beach to dry—after which Mrs. Vessey began the task of washing out the encrusted salt.

On our next trip we pushed through to the galley and

brought out seven bottles of liquor and all the tinned food we could find—some bully beef, several kinds of fruit, some tinned butter and even cream. Once we had carried the food ashore, we washed the tins four or five times in fresh water to get rid of every particle of salt, then dried them all thoroughly before storing them away.

Towards the beginning of the second week I finally did discover Mrs. Vessey's cigarettes—two very soggy red and white cartons of Pall Mall—and I will never forget her expression as I handed them over to her.

"It's not the end of the world," I said consolingly. "You'll have to unwrap them, then put the tobacco in fresh water to wash away the salt. After that, dry it, and I'll give you some of my cigarette papers so you can roll new cigarettes."

Poor Mrs. Vessey! The haunting vision of a good smoke now her precious cigarettes were actually in front of her was strong enough to overcome any temporary dismay. Hoping for a miracle, she grabbed the dripping cartons and tore them open.

And, do you know, incredible though it was, there *were* some dry cigarettes. Five packets in individual Cellophane covers had managed to escape the general soaking and were dry enough for us to smoke right away. Indeed, a cigarette had appeared in the corner of Mrs. Vessey's mouth before I had recovered from the shock. Of all the unusual occurrences on Suvarov, this was surely one of the most astonishing. Those cigarettes had been in salt water for a week.

She was so delighted she gave me two of the dry packets—but I wasn't going to light up immediately! I broke one open and rolled half the tobacco in one of my own papers.

My next triumph was the day I discovered Ed's teeth. Ever since the water in the cabin had become thick and foul, I had despaired of ever locating such a small (though precious) prize. By this time there was very little of value left to salvage, but one morning I was holding myself down with one hand and scraping the other along the floor through the sodden mass of papers when my fist closed on a hard, curiously shaped object.

These indeed proved to be his snappers, and how we celebrated that night! I remember I had prepared a fowl that morning and for the first time since the wreck of the *Tiburon*, Ed was able to get his teeth into something solid! We opened a tin of peaches and a bottle of rum, both salvaged from the yacht, and as supper ended, Ed toasted me and cried, "Thanks, Tom! And I'll never complain again if they hurt me. From now on these teeth are staying right where they are."

Our celebration kept us up much later than usual that night. We killed most of the bottle of rum whilst Mrs. Vessey played her guitar by the light of the hurrican lamp. Towards midnight I made a remark which was to produce astonishing results. "Time to turn in," I said. "Kerosene's precious in this part of the world."

"Hell, Tom," Ed apologised, immediately full of contrition, "I hate to think of us using all that stuff of yours just for a sing-sing."

The next morning he returned from a walk on the beach looking very thoughtful. Soon he cornered me in the shed at the bottom of the yard where I was stacking firewood. "This may sound crazy," he began hesitantly "but I think if you can help me, I can fix us up with electric light."

I looked at him stupefied.

"Yeah, I mean it. I've got a generator, an engine, plenty of electrical fittings—and fuel. All we've got to do is bring 'em ashore. Once we've dried it out there's no reason why we shouldn't be able to start up the motor."

As soon as it was low tide we rowed out to the wreck. The engine that drove the generator was bolted down at each of its four corners to the deck aft of the wheel. It must have weighed at least three hundred pounds.

Since the bottom half was permanently submerged, the only way we could get at the bolts was to kneel on the afterdeck armed with a big spanner, lean forward with the water almost washing our faces and try to unscrew the nuts on the bolts. It proved a painstaking job. It took us almost a day to unscrew three of the nuts, but when we came to the fourth we just couldn't get a spanner round it. We tried for another whole day but, constantly forced to work with our hands underwater all the time, it was impossible to shift it.

"We just can't give up now," exclaimed Ed in a frenzy of frustration. "Let's cut through the bolt with a hacksaw."

In theory this sounded fine, but when we came to try, we found we couldn't manoeuvre the hacksaw itself close enough to let us get at the bolt. In the end we were forced to remove the blade from the hacksaw and eventually we cut through that bolt like two prisoners painfully whittling away at the bars of a cell window. Working alternately, always underwater, this laborious job took us another day before we finally freed the motor.

Even then it was too heavy to lift between us. Fortunately, however, the masts were still standing, so, wading knee-deep in water, we rigged up a home-made block and tackle, hoisted the engine off the deck and then lowered it gently into the stern of my boat. Then we dropped overboard two rubber emergency tanks of diesel fuel which Ed carried on deck, and which we hadn't bothered to salvage before, and towed them back to the island.

Once we had the engine on the beach we started to

take it to pieces and wash each section thoroughly with oil to free it from salt water. It was a backbreaking job working on the beach under the hot glare of the sun; and after nearly a month under the water every nut and bolt seemed to be jammed and encrusted with salt.

For four days we worked on it, often becoming so absorbed in our task we even forgot about meals until Sileia came running down to the beach to announce that supper was ready. The entire motor was covered with a thick scum which soon dirtied all my precious tools. Once we had uncovered the cylinder the procedure was fairly simple, but until that moment we had not dared to cut our way through any of the bolts as we had no spare parts. However, we did risk a few sharp, oblique taps with a hammer and chisel to loosen the most obstinate before we got down to the pistons and valves.

After we had washed each part in kerosene and dried it out, we re-assembled the motor and filled her with fuel. I stood watching—hardly able to believe it would work. Ed gave the flywheel a pull. Nothing happened. Another turn, another heave. Still nothing.

"But I can feel her—she's almost starting," grunted Ed.

He gave one more huge turn to the flywheel and this time the pistons moved. She spluttered, hesitated and then throbbed into life.

Triumphantly Ed leaned over and switched it off and we changed the oil again. We did this four times— running the engine for only half a minute—before Ed was satisfied.

While Ed worked on one of his two spare generators, I cut down four branches of tahuna to serve as rollers so that we could transport the motor from the beach to the shack. After peeling off the bark they functioned well enough, though once we were ready for the journey, it took us the best part of another day to roll the engine to a level spot near the shack, where the coast-watchers had made a concrete base for *their* generator years before.

The engine should have been bolted down, of course, but as we had no means of doing this we built a wooden frame and drove in wedges designed to hold the motor secure enough to prevent any undue vibration. By this time we had salvaged all the lighting fixtures we could from the boat, and by the next afternoon Ed had festooned the bedroom, kai room, even the cook-house with wires.

In all, we were the proud possessors of four light bulbs, and on that memorable day, just as dusk was approaching, Ed started up the engine. I remember I was standing on the veranda with Mrs. Vessey—who, by now, had smoked all her cigarettes and was back to rolled banana leaves—when Ed shouted, "Now for it, Tom!"

He gave the flywheel a couple of turns and within a few seconds Suvarov was ablaze—well nearly!—with electric light.

As I wrote in my journal that night by electric light, "None of those people down in Raro would believe me if I told them I'd got electric light on Suvarov." Then for some reason I added, "It's all very nice—if only it didn't remind me of the civilisation from which I've always wanted to escape."

Looking back on the months my castaways stayed with me, I am still astonished not only that a harsh word never passed between us, but also at the remarkable way they all seemed to settle down and develop a philosophy which saw them through with never a hint of complaint or discontent.

It was different for me—I had chosen this existence. And, in a way, too, Mrs. Vessey's Samoan attitude to life probably helped her to accept what had happened. But for Ed the loss of the *Tiburon* must have been heartbreaking, and the prospect of facing months without any sort of contact with civilisation must have been desperately worrying and frustrating. But Ed was a remarkable man. He never grumbled, he never ever gave the *appearance* of being worried. And it was only when they were rescued and he was no longer able to contain his excitement, that I began to realise that all this time he had been concealing his anxieties in order not to disturb his wife and daughter.

His release was not to be granted for over two months, during which time we had settled down to a pleasant routine. Then, one morning at eight o'clock, as I was walking along the beach I spotted the grey outline of a vessel five miles or so out to sea.

She was north of the island and travelling eastwards. Even at that distance, I felt sure she must be a navy ship.

Running back along the path, I shouted, "Ed, come down here quick and bring your binoculars!"

Instinctively he knew what had happened. "Coming!" he yelled excitedly, and within a minute or so had reached me on the pier, only to see the ship disappearing behind the north point of the island.

"My God!" he gasped, lowering the binoculars. "We've got to stop her—we've *got* to."

"I'm afraid it's too late," I muttered.

Ed's wife and daughter came running up as Ed cried, "Let's go to the other side of the island."

It was only three hundred yards across Suvarov from the pier to Pylades Bay, but never had it seemed to take so long. Ed charged ahead, oblivious of the low branches and undergrowth, panting with the sudden exertion, while his wife trailed behind crying, "Wait for me!" as though she were going to be lost.

"We might still see it," grunted Ed. "Tom—we've *got* to stop her."

We broke out of the jungle into the sunlight of the beach—and there she was, right ahead of us.

"She's a naval vessel all right," Ed said from behind the binoculars, adding in a strangled, choked voice, "but I don't think she's going to stop."

I had not the heart to tell him that from my own experience he was entirely right. But Ed was not to be beaten. Turning to Sileia, he cried, "Run quickly and get your mother's mirror from the bedroom." He looked at me anxiously as she raced away. "Maybe we can flash a message. There's still time."

In less than two minutes Sileia was back. Ed grabbed the mirror from her, and began to use it as a heliograph.

"You keep an eye on her, Tom," he said as he kept on signalling by catching the rays of the sun. I took the binoculars, raised them to my eyes and saw that she was steaming steadily on course. And then suddenly it seemed to me that she was *not*—and that she had stopped moving.

"Anything happened?" asked Ed.

It *looked* as though the vessel had stopped, but I couldn't be sure. Maybe my eyes were playing tricks and I dared not bring myself to hold out any false hopes. "Keep signalling," I grunted.

Within two minutes, however, I was quite certain. "She's spotted your signals!" I shouted excitedly.

On hearing my words he dropped the mirror, forgetting I was there, and lifting Sileia up in his arms, cried, "We're saved, darling—do you realise it?—we're saved!"

Through the binoculars I could now see clearly that the vessel had already changed course. In a few minutes she was heading straight for the island. Within the hour she was anchored in the lagoon, and Ed and I rowed out to board her. She was a New Zealand frigate, the *Pukaki*.

We climbed aboard and the captain, after telling us how he had seen the signals, obligingly agreed to wait for Ed to pack his stuff and even sent a shore party to help load up the heavier items like the generator and motor— for Ed wanted to take everything he had salvaged from his yacht; these were all he possessed in the world. "But you'll have to get a move on," said the skipper sternly. "I can't afford to wait all day."

I stayed on board a little longer talking to the young New Zealanders amongst the crew, who reminded me vividly of the eagerness and enthusiasm with which I had started out on a similar life. I didn't want to be with the Vesseys who were ashore packing up their things, for their imminent departure was already affecting me more deeply than any previous leave-taking I had known. As I lingered on board I was dreading to see them leave. We had been through so much together, lived as close as most human beings can get, with never a cross word between us, and in my own fatherly way I had become very fond of Sileia. With something of a shock, I realised that I had been secretly hoping that maybe they would never be rescued.

Fortunately naval procedure seldom permits one time for protracted farewells.

I was grateful for this. We said our good-byes in the small cabin which the captain had allotted them. Ed shook my hand, I gave Sileia a hug, and then Mrs. Vessey—jolly banana-smoking Mrs. Vessey—started weeping, threw her arms around my neck and kissed me fervently. "God bless you, Tom," was all she said, "for what you've done."

I vanished over the side into my boat pretty smartly because the prickly feeling in my eyes was threatening to betray me. As I started rowing for the shore, I remember saying almost savagely to myself, "Dammit, Neale—you've chosen your life—don't spoil it."

Long before I beached the boat, the *Pukaki* was on her way. I have never seen Ed and his family again.

Postscript

WELL, THAT IS the end of my story, for I left Suvarov on December 27, 1963, barely two months after the castaways had been rescued, and a variety of circumstances contributed to my decision.

The predominant reason was a very simple one. I realised I was getting on, and the prospect of a lonely death did not particularly appeal to me. I wasn't being sentimental about it, but the time had come to wake up from an exquisite dream before it turned into a nightmare.

I might have lingered on the island for a few more years, but soon after the Vesseys left, a party of eleven pearl divers descended on Suvarov—and, frankly, turned my heaven into hell. They were happy-go-lucky Manihiki natives, and I didn't dislike them, but their untidiness, noise, and close proximity were enough to dispel any wavering doubts I might have had. Then, when I heard that more natives might be coming to dive for a couple of months each year in the lagoon, I resolved to leave with the divers.

I did so—and I have not regretted the decision. I am back in Raro now, and you know, having proved my point—that I *could* make a go of it on a desert island and be happy alone—store-keeping doesn't after all seem such a monotonous job as it did in the years before 1952.

I have a wealth of memories that no man can take away from me and which I have enjoyed recalling in these pages. I hope you have enjoyed them too.